Guide To

DERECH
ERETZ

Contents

Introduction

The mastery of any discipline can only be attained by continuous study and practice. Such devoted application is certainly necessary in order to become proficient in the laws of the *Shulchan Aruch* and to refine one's personality. Unfortunately, few people apply themselves with the same dedication towards reaching perfection in *derech eretz*.

In actuality, it is impossible to attain *derech eretz* unless one studies this subject with the same intensity as he would study the *Shulchan Aruch* or any other discipline. This is implied by the statement of the Sages, "The daughters of Tzlafchad were wise." Rashbam writes that they were wise in *derech eretz* (*Bava Basra* 119a). This explanation reveals that the Torah considers *derech eretz* to be a wisdom. As with all wisdoms, it can be mastered only through careful study and meticulous discipline.

Any person, even a *talmid chacham*, who believes that he is capable of behaving with *derech eretz* simply by relying on his own judgment is making an essential mistake.

This work is based on sources from the Talmud, Midrash, and other classic works.

This book originally appeared in Hebrew under the title *Darchei Noam* (*Ways of Pleasantness*). It was inspired by the verse: "Its ways [the ways of the Torah] are ways of pleasantness and all its paths are peace" (Mishlei 3:17). For a person who behaves with *derech eretz* radiates a sense of peace and harmony, and inspires others to behave in a similar manner. This is the intention of the Sages' statement, "The only vessel able to hold blessing is Shalom" (end of *Uktzin*), and *derech eretz* leads to Shalom.

We hope that the study of this volume will be beneficial to those who strive to acquire the trait of *derech eretz*.

Preface

Derech Eretz

Elemental *Derech Eretz*

Derech eretz can be defined as a type of behavior that will be acceptable by one's society and which is geared towards making people happy, as the Mishnah says: "Which is the proper path one should choose? One that is pleasing to the one who performs it and is pleasing to others" (*Avos* 2:1).

The essential ingredients of *derech eretz* are: impartiality; humility; sensitivity towards the feelings and rights of others; an understanding of human nature; a sense of justice; and respect for each individual and for humanity as a whole.

Derech eretz requires a discipline of kindness, cheerfulness and constant awareness of one's surroundings. Acting with *derech eretz* (besides being a virtue in its own right) leads to peaceful co-existence with one's family, neighbors and society, and avoids the multitudes of misunderstandings caused by the behavior and attitudes of those who are lacking in this respect.

Tanna Devei Eliyahu (*Ravah* 11) states: "Even when the Jewish people do not fulfill any Torah principle other than *derech eretz*, the verse, 'Five of you shall chase one hundred, and one hundred of you shall chase ten thousand' (Vayikra 26:8) will be realized. If they do fulfill the principles of the Torah and perform the mitzvos, then the verse, 'One shall chase one thousand and two shall chase ten thousand' (Devarim 32:30) will come true." This statement implies that *derech eretz* is a redeeming virtue even when the Jewish people do not fulfill the other precepts of the Torah.

The *Yalkut* (Bereishis, end of ch. 3) also writes about this concept: "*Derech eretz* preceded the giving of the Torah by twenty-six generations,[1] as the verse says, ... 'and He placed at the east of Gan Eden...the revolving sword to guard the way of the Tree of Life' (Bereishis 3:24) [The word, 'the way' ('*derech*'), refers to *derech eretz*]." Here we see that an aspect of *derech eretz* existed in the world even before the Torah was given to the Jewish people; it is a mode of behavior crucial to the existence of humanity. A person who lacks this trait falls short of fulfilling his quintessential role as a human being.

Even people who do not have fear of Heaven can understand the importance of elemental *derech eretz*. This was demonstrated by the Philistines when they returned the holy Ark they had captured from the Israel-

---

1. There were twenty-six generations from Adam until Moshe.

ites, as related in Shmuel (I ch. 6): "And they [the priests] said: 'If you will send the Ark of the God of Yisrael, do not send it empty.' " The Philistines perceived that the Ark deserved an honorable procession; thus, they sent gold and silver artifacts to adorn it. *Tanna Devei Eliyahu* comments: "Although they were priests to idolatry, they had *derech eretz*" (*Eliyahu Rabbah*, ch. 11). This concept is repeated again in *Tanna Devei Eliyahu*: "Although the generation of the First Temple were guilty of idolatry, they merited to be redeemed from exile because they had *derech eretz*, gave charity and performed kind deeds" (ibid. ch. 14).

Derech Eretz as Defined by the Torah

The Torah obligates a Jew in more than elemental *derech eretz*; he must attain a more sublime, Torah-prescribed mode of behavior. This is the meaning of the often quoted expression of Chazal, "The *Torah* teaches *derech eretz*."

For example, the commentaries explain the verse, "Let Us make Adam" (Bereishis 1:26) to mean that Hashem took counsel with the angels before creating man; this teaches us that a person of distinction should always take counsel with people of lesser stature. We also learn that a Rav should honor his disciples from the verse, "Choose for *us* men..." (Shemos 17:9). Here Moshe Rabbeinu charged Yehoshua to choose suitable men for Moshe, yet used the expression of "*us*" to include also Yehoshua his pupil. Were it not for these verses, we would be lacking in our understanding of the proper behavior of a Rav towards his disciples.

Even a *talmid chacham* should not assume that his Torah knowledge will automatically lead him to behave with *derech eretz*. He should always bear in mind what our Sages said, "A *talmid chacham* who does not have the sense to act with *derech eretz* is worse than a dead animal" (*Vayikra Rabbah* 1:15). This point is illustrated by the Talmud's account of the final moments of R. Yochanan Ben Zakkai's life (*Berachos* 28b): "When his disciples visited him moments before his death, he began to cry. They said to him, '[The] light of Yisrael, [the] right pillar, [the] powerful hammer, why do you cry?' He answered them, '...there are two paths in front of me, one leads to Gan Eden and one to *Gehinnom*; I do not know to which path they will lead me. Should I not cry?!' "

The question remains: Why did R. Yochanan Ben Zakkai consider the possibility that he would be led to *Gehinnom*? This is the man about whom the Talmud reports: "He studied every section of the Torah" (*Sukkah* 28a). He was responsible for saving Yavne and her Sages, and he was Israel's spiritual guide for forty years following the destruction of the Temple. What fault could he have perceived within himself?

Unlike the laws of the *Shulchan Aruch*, a person can never fully determine whether he has satisfactorily fulfilled his obligation to behave with *derech eretz* in his interpersonal affairs. Due to people's individuality, it is not possible to apply the rules of behavior equally in all situations. One person may expect more honor than others. Another may consider a tone of voice commonly used by people to be offensive. Perhaps this was R. Yochanan Ben Zakkai's fear. He realized that it is impossible for one to determine whether his mode of behavior is satisfactory until he is judged by the Heavenly Court after death, and that a person's Torah knowledge cannot guarantee his ability to behave with *derech eretz*.

This diversity of human nature requires a versatile approach so as to live in peace and harmony with everyone. Furthermore, the situations of life are manifold and often change without a moment's notice. Knowing how to act or to respond in any given situation would be an impossible task without prior preparation and training. This book discusses as many life situations as possible, so as to give the student a clear guide and a sound basis to enable him to act with readiness in any situation.

Chapter 1

Interpersonal Relations

The Mishnah states, "Welcome every person with a pleasing countenance" (*Avos* 1:15). Rambam comments, "One is obligated to conduct his affairs with others in a gentle and pleasing manner." Rabbeinu Yonah writes in a similar vein: "One should conduct himself in such a way as to cause others to feel satisfaction from the relationship, by bending his will for the sake of others. He who is able to act in such a manner will certainly acquire many devoted friends." Both Rambam's and Rabbeinu Yonah's explanations stress the same point: a person's code of behavior must be deemed acceptable by society. This is the essential obligation of *derech eretz*.

At this point one might wonder, "Why must I concern myself with other people's opinions? Is it not enough if I know my behavior is correct?" The answer to this question is twofold:

First, various Mishnaic and Talmudic sources stress the importance of behaving in a manner deemed acceptable by one's society. For example, our Sages state, "One's perspectives must always be in tune with those of society" (*Kesuvos* 17a). This obligation is repeated in *Pirkei Avos*: "Which is the proper path one should choose? One that is pleasing to the one who performs it and is pleasing to others" (*Avos* 2:1). Another example is the statement, "One who is well liked by people is regarded favorably by Hashem" (*Avos* 3:10).

Second, one who behaves in an exemplary manner sanctifies the name of Hashem. Our Sages explain the verse, "And you will love Hashem your God..." (Devarim 6:4) in the following way: "One must study and teach, as well as speak gently to people and conduct his affairs with them in an honorable manner. When people see such a person, what do they say? Happy is he who studies Torah, happy is his father who taught him Torah, happy is his rebbi who taught him Torah; pitiful are those who do not study Torah. Look at so and so who studied Torah. How pleasant and beautiful are his deeds, how perfect his ways. The verse 'Yisrael, through whom I will be praised' refers to such a person" (*Yoma* 86a).

Chapter 2

Welcoming Others with a Pleasing Countenance

"The Mishnah states, 'Welcome every person with a pleasing countenance' [*Avos* 1:15]. What is the essence of this message? It teaches that if one presents even the most precious gift to someone while maintaining an unpleasant facial expression, it is considered as if he gave nothing. Conversely, if one merely welcomes another person with a pleasing countenance, it is considered as if he gave him the most precious gift in the world, even if he did not give him anything" (*Avos deRav Nasan* 13:12). Rambam comments that one who welcomes another person *in a joyful manner* fulfills the Mishnah's rule to an even greater extent, since this type of reception will make him feel truly at ease.

It is apparent from this Mishnah that the Sages recognized the important role that facial expressions play in interpersonal relations. People receive numerous signals, both explicit and implicit, that gauge the degree of affection with which others regard them. The most revealing of these signals is facial expression. One who is not consciously aware of his facial expressions may be guilty of transmitting wrong signals; if his affection for another person is not sufficiently reflected by his facial expression, he is liable to lose that relationship. The other person will consciously or subconsciously pick up unfriendly signals, which will in turn cause him to withdraw from the relationship.

The ideal tool for expressing affection is the face. One who masters the art of pleasant facial expressions will benefit himself and others, while one who continues to allow his facial expression to involuntarily betray his emotions will cause untold damage to himself and his acquaintances. This is the intention of the Sages' statement, " 'Teeth are whiter than milk' [Bereishis 49:12]. It is better to show the white of one's teeth [by smiling] to a friend than to give him milk to drink" (*Kesuvos* 111b). A smile can sometimes provide more nourishment than food!

This skill is absolutely essential for a teacher, regardless of whether his students are children or adults. As the Sages say, "If you find a student who has difficulty with his studies, attribute it to his teacher's failure to show a pleasing countenance" (*Taanis* 8a).

The *Shulchan Aruch* dictates that *tzedakah* must be given with a friendly demeanor. In addition, the donor should offer words of encouragement and comfort to the poor person and thereby alleviate his sorrow. One who gives *tzedakah* gruffly or while maintaining an unfriendly expression loses the merit of the mitzvah. In fact, the Sages consider the act of comforting a poor person more important than giving him money: "One who gives a *perutah* to a poor person is blessed with six blessings, while one who offers him words of encouragement is blessed with eleven blessings." The verse says, "And if you draw out your soul to the hungry, and satisfy the afflicted soul..." Rashi explains that this refers to offering words of encouragement to a poor person. The verse then lists the eleven rewards one receives for this act: "...[1]then shall your light rise in darkness, [2]and your gloom be as the noonday. [3]And Hashem shall guide you continually, [4]and satisfy your soul in drought, [5]and make strong your bones [6]and you shall be like a watered garden [7]and like a spring of water, whose waters fail not. [8]And they that shall be of you shall build the ruins; [9]you shall raise up the foundations of many generations, [10]and you shall be called 'the repairer of the breach,' [11]'the restorer of paths to dwell in' " (Yeshayahu 58:10-12).

To Act Gently

"One should be soft as a reed, not hard as a cedar tree" (*Taanis* 20b). This statement teaches that one must always speak gently, even when feeling agitated and irritable. This is an extremely difficult task, considering that even a spiritual giant such as Yaakov Avinu did not attain the highest level of this ability: The Torah relates that Rachel asked of Yaakov, "...give me children.... And Yaakov became angry and he said, 'Am I like God that I have withheld children from you?' " (Bereishis 19:2). Our Sages comment that Yaakov's response was inappropriate: "Is this how one responds to a suffering person? Your punishment will be that your children [born by Leah] will stand up before her [Rachel's] children [meaning that Leah's children will stand up before Yosef]!" (*Midrash Rabbah* 71:6).

A person who studies Torah must take special care not to manifest his superiority over others by haughty language. The Talmud reports that a man once came back from his Rav's house and felt haughty after his study session. Consequently, he was rude to another person, from whom he eventually had to ask forgiveness. Following this incident, the man taught others, "One must always be as soft as a reed..." (*Taanis* 20b).

Saying Shalom:
Acknowledging Another's Presence

"One must offer greetings to his family, acquaintances, strangers and even non-Jews. It is said of R. Yochanan Ben Zakkai that no one ever preceded him in offering greetings, even a non-Jew in the marketplace" (*Berachos 17a*). Yet, the Talmud says about R. Yochanan, "He never walked four *amos* without Torah and tefillin" (*Sukkah* 28a); his mind was constantly preoccupied with Torah study. Why would R. Yochanan interrupt his thoughts in order to extend greetings to a non-Jew? The answer may well be that he understood that extending greetings to others promotes peaceful relations between people. He considered the momentary interruption of Torah study a worthy investment for promoting peaceful coexistence between Jews and non-Jews.

Maharal writes that one must offer greetings even to a willful transgressor of sins — otherwise the sinner will wrongly conclude that the Torah advocates scorning ignorant people. This in effect profanes the name of God.

Welcoming a Guest

It is customary to greet a visitor by saying, *"Shalom aleichem!"* This fulfills the rule, "Extend greetings to every man, as it says, 'Ask for peace and pursue it' " (Tehillim 34:15). Greeting a guest in this manner makes him feel welcome. One must also educate his children to greet a guest with *"Shalom aleichem!"*

The importance of extending greetings to others is illustrated by the following rule: "If one who dreams that he was excommunicated cannot find ten *talmidei chachamim* to annul the decree, he should sit by the road and say *'shalom'* to passersby" (*Nedarim* 8a). Rabbeinu Nissim explains that saying *shalom* to others will prompt them to respond in the same manner; this will protect him from misfortune. This explanation teaches that one who extends greetings to others derives direct benefit for himself.

Returning a Greeting

"One who is greeted by a fellow Jew and does not return the greeting is considered a thief" (*Berachos* 6b). The *Shulchan Aruch* also underscores the importance of returning a greeting. According to *halachah*, it is permitted to interrupt the recital of *Shema* in order to return any person's greeting (*Mishnah Berurah* 66:2). (This does not apply nowadays since we are accustomed to not interrupting in the middle of davening.)

Chapter 3

Bending One's Will for the Sake of Others

The essential reason for most quarrels is a basic human shortcoming: it is extremely difficult for people to accept opinions that differ from their own. Rabbeinu Asher writes, "Do not be unyielding, but rather, bend your will for the sake of others" (*Orchos Chaim*). This quality is exemplified by Rachel Imeinu, who informed her sister Leah of the secret signs that Yaakov would use in order to identify his chosen wife Rachel (as Yaakov suspected that Lavan might exchange Leah for Rachel.) By doing this she saved Leah from shame and embarrassment, but lost her chosen fiancé Yaakov (*Derech Eretz Zuta*, ch. 1).

Everyone Is Different

The inherent obstacle in putting this concept into practice is that values and opinions vary from one individual to the next; as the Sages say, "People's opinions are as diverse as their facial features" (*Midrash Rabbah*, Bemidbar 21:2). Moshe Rabbeinu attached enormous importance to the quality of leaders being understanding of people, as expressed in the verse, "May Hashem, the God of all spirits and of all flesh, appoint a person to lead the congregation" (Bemidbar 27:15). The Midrash explains that Moshe prayed that his successor be endowed with the ability to understand and tolerate each Jew's personality (*Tanchumah, Parashas Pinchas*). *Yalkut Shimoni* offers a similar interpretation, explaining that Moshe prayed that his successor's soul be large enough to accommodate the differing personalities of six hundred thousand souls, a quality he deemed essential for the future leader of the Jewish people. (This quality will also be shared by the *Moshiach*.)

The Rashba explains that the reason why the Sages stressed that "people's opinions differ" is in order to emphasize one's obligation to accept opinions which differ from one's own.

Humility — Prerequisite of Tolerance

Masseches Derech Eretz describes the degree of humility one should strive to achieve: "Be as the threshold, upon which everyone treads, and as the peg, which people use for hanging objects" (*Derech Eretz Zuta*, ch. 1). This means that one is obligated to tolerate others even if they do not consider him worthy of respect. The Midrash adds, "Be lowly before everyone, especially before members of your household.... Be as the threshold, upon which everyone treads, for eventually the house will collapse, but the threshold will remain untouched" (ibid. ch. 3).

The Midrash says, "Everyone should learn from Moshe Rabbeinu: He said, 'Choose for *us* people...' (Shemos 18:15). This teaches that he considered his pupil [Yehoshua] as important as himself." The Midrash develops a similar idea: "From where do we learn that one must treat others with as much respect as he treats his teacher? From the verse, 'And Aharon said to Moshe, "Please, my master..." ' (Bemidbar 12:11). Aharon was Moshe Rabbeinu's elder brother, and yet he addressed him as 'my master.' This teaches us that he regarded him as his Rav" (*Yalkut* Shemos 264).

Tolerance leads to peace and to new friendships, and precludes anger.

"A pious man was once asked, 'To what do you attribute people's affection for you?' He answered, 'Because I always consider other people to be better than I' " (*Orchos Tzaddikim, Shaar Haanavah*).

Chapter 4

Fulfilling Another's Need

The essential purpose of performing kind deeds is to fulfill another's need and to alleviate his discomfort. Yet different people have vastly different needs. A clear understanding of what a particular individual's needs are can only be attained by someone who really cares for and empathizes with that person. Many people are very willing to extend the kind of help they feel they want to give; few concern themselves with providing the kind of help the individual requires. This idea is emphasized in *Mesillas Yesharim*: "One must try to please others as much as possible, whether by showing him respect or in any other manner; it is a *mitzvah* of piety to perform an act *which one knows will please another person*" (ch. 17).

This concept is apparent in Talmudic sources. For example, R. Elazar said, "The merit one receives for performing *tzedakah* is proportional to the degree of *chessed* [kindness] one has extended" (*Sukkah* 49b). Rashi explains that the act of giving charity is considered *tzedakah*, and the effort one expends in order to offer the poor person the full benefit of the charity is considered *chessed*. For example, bringing money to the poor person's home rather than waiting until he asks for it, or providing for him an article which he needs very much is considered *chessed*. In conclusion, Rashi says that *chessed* is an act which indicates that *the giver has taken into account the best interests of the needy person.*

It is told that one of R. Yisrael Salanter's disciples once complained to him that his efforts to do *chessed* for his wife were not appreciated by her. R. Yisrael responded, "Know that performing an act that you think is beneficial for your wife, or giving her something that you think she is lacking, is not yet considered *chessed*; rather, *chessed* is the performance of an act that *she* considers beneficial, the giving of something that *she* feels she is lacking."

A practical application of this concept is the following case: If one gives an article of clothing to a poor person and the color or style is not to his liking, the donor is considered to have given away his property in vain — he has not fulfilled the poor person's need for suitable clothes. In such a case, the donor should not even expect an expression of gratitude from the poor person. Furthermore, by giving the poor person an inappropriate article of clothing, the donor has put him in an uncomfortable position, thus augmenting his sorrow. Needless to say, it would be a show of appreciation on the recipient's part to express his gratitude regardless of whether or not the object is appropriate.

An essential principle to keep in mind while doing *chessed* is that a good intention does not redeem an inappropriate act. This is demonstrated by the following occurrence, related in *Avos deRav Nasan* (48:1): "R. Shimon Ben Yochai went to visit a leper who suffered many afflictions. Due to his great pain he cursed God, and R. Shimon Ben Yochai rebuked him for doing so. After the rebuke, the leper said, 'May it be His will that my leprosy should afflict you.' " Yavetz writes that R. Shimon Ben Yochai accepted this curse because he recognized that he was at fault, for the Sages say that one should not try to console a person who has experienced suffering while the sufferer feels angry.

Chapter 5

Order of Priority in Chessed

Derech eretz demands that *chessed* be allocated to the right people. *Mishpat Tzedek* writes in the name of R. Yoel that if a person who does *chessed* shows preference for helping other needy people over his own relatives, it indicates that his intentions are not purely for the sake of Heaven, for relatives must receive one's first consideration. The following list outlines the priorities of extending *chessed*, in descending order:

1) One who lacks a basic necessity takes precedence over a person whose lack is less vital, e.g., providing food for the hungry takes precedence over providing clothing for the needy.

2) Since it is less becoming for a woman to knock on doors and ask for charity, a female in need of charity takes precedence over a male. *Sifsei Kohen* writes that this rule applies even if a particular woman is accustomed to knocking on doors to ask for charity.

3) If a group of poor people of equal standing come

to ask for charity and one does not have enough money to give them all, a Kohen takes precedence over a Levi and a Levi takes precedence over a Yisrael. If one of the individuals is superior in Torah knowledge, he takes precedence over the others. One's rebbe takes precedence over other *talmidei chachamim* (*Yoreh Deah*, ch. 251).

Relatives

4) The above order concerns individuals who are not relatives. The following list outlines the order of priorities for extending *chessed* to relatives, in descending order:

a) One's wife, whom the Sages say is considered as her husband's own body, takes precedence over all other relatives.

b) One's children under the age of six.

c) One's parents; one's father takes precedence over one's mother.

d) One's grandparents; paternal grandparents take precedence over maternal grandparents.

e) One's children over the age of six.

Some authorities are of the opinion that grandchildren should be considered as one's children, who are given priority over one's brothers and sisters. This rule does not include the children of one's daughter.

f) One's siblings; a brother or sister from the father's side takes precedence over a brother or sister from the mother's side.

g) One's paternal uncle and aunt.

h) One's maternal uncle and aunt.

5) Relatives take precedence over other people.

Who exactly is considered a "relative" in terms of

receiving a priority allotment of *tzedakah* is discussed at length in the responsa volume of the Chasam Sofer on *Choshen Mishpat*, chapters 121 and 127. He concludes that any relative who would be disqualified as a valid witness, e.g., a first cousin, is also considered a relative as regards priority for receiving charity. Any relation whom people commonly perceive as a relative, e.g., people who are referred to as "relatives" in one's will, even a fourth cousin, would also be considered a relative (but not relations on one's wife's side).

6) A person living in one's house takes precedence over his neighbor. A neighbor does not necessarily refer to a person who lives in one's neighborhood — even someone with whom one socializes or with whom one has business connections is considered his neighbor (*Sefer Me'ir Einaim, Choshen Mishpat* 253:66).

7) One's neighbor takes precedence over other residents of his city.

8) Residents of one's city take precedence over needy people from a different city. This rule applies even if the resident of his city is an ignorant person and the needy person from a different city is a *talmid chacham* (*Yoreh Deah* 251:3, *Choshen Mishpat* 253:29).

9) Some authorities are of the opinion that the relatives of one's wife who live in another city are accorded the same degree of priority as are the residents of one's own city. According to this opinion, the gift one allocates to his wife's relatives should be one third that which he would allocate to his own relatives. (*Pitchei Teshuvah, Yoreh De'ah* 251:2).

Further Priorities

One is obligated to do *chessed* for a person he dislikes before doing so for a person he loves. It is questionable whether a person whom one dislikes takes precedence over one's relative (*Ahavas Chessed*, sec. 1, ch. 4).

In general, a person who suffers more anguish than others from his lack, or who is handicapped in other ways, should be given first priority for receiving charity. By being sensitive to individual needs, one multiplies the quality of the *chessed* one is doing. This only applies if the individuals are equal in every other regard, that is, they are both from the same city or they are both one's relatives. This rule is derived from the Torah's admonishment concerning the manner in which one should behave towards an orphan and a widow. Since a widow suffers more anguish than an orphan, she is more deserving of charity; an orphan in turn takes precedence over other needy people who are not orphans (this idea is discussed further in *Ahavas Chessed*, ch. 6).

Chapter 6

The Obligation to Integrate into Society

The Talmud dictates that "One must always integrate with people" (*Kesuvos* 16b, 17). The various interpretations of this statement can be categorized into three basic approaches:

Conducting Essential Interpersonal Relations

Mesillas Yesharim explains, "A person should befriend upstanding people for short periods of time, to enable himself to study Torah and make a living; no more than this is necessary." According to this understanding, the Talmud's rule, "A person must integrate with people," teaches that one should not isolate himself from people entirely, since certain necessary functions can only be fulfilled through interaction with others.

Even so, one must employ careful scrutiny in selecting appropriate individuals with whom to conduct such vital relationships.

Offering Support and Encouragement

The Talmud asks, "How should one dance in front of the bride? *Beis Hillel* said, 'One should declare in the presence of every bride, "Beautiful and charming bride!"' *Beis Shammai* said to *Beis Hillel*, 'If she is ugly or blind do we say to her, "Beautiful and charming bride!"'? The Torah says, "Distance yourself from untruthful words!"' *Beis Hillel* said to *Beis Shammai*, 'According to you, if a person made an unwise purchase in the market, should one praise him for having purchased the object, or ridicule him? We must say that one must praise him. About this the *Chachamim* say, "One must always integrate with people"'" (*Kesuvos* 17a).

This implies that there is no prohibition against bending the truth, if one does so for the sake of *derech eretz*. *Yalkut HaGaonim* writes that *derech eretz* dictates that one must praise a person's purchase, since otherwise the person will feel sad (*Shitah Mekubetzes*). Rashi explains that the statement, "One must always integrate with people," means that "one must fulfill the will of every person." *Shitah Mekubetzes* explains that one is obligated to praise every person even though his actions are not entirely praiseworthy. This has the vital effect of making a person feel happy and content.

Conforming to Custom

It is stated in *Masseches Derech Eretz* (*Zuta*, ch. 5): "A person should not be awake amongst those who are sleeping, nor sleeping amongst those who are awake; cry amongst those who laugh, nor laugh amongst those who cry; sit amongst those who stand, nor stand amongst those who sit; he should not study Written Torah amongst those studying Oral Torah, and he should not study Oral Torah amongst those studying Written Torah. In general, a person's behavior should not be at variance with other people's behavior." This idea is derived from Moshe Rabbeinu's example, as R. Tanchum Ben Chanilai said, "A person should not deviate from the custom — Moshe ascended to the Heavens and he did not eat bread; the angels descended [to visit Avraham Avinu] and they did eat bread" (*Bava Metzia* 86b).

This concept has halachic ramifications. The Mishnah states: "In a city where the custom is to work on *erev Pesach* until noon, work may be performed. In a city where the custom is not to work, work may not be performed. One who travels from a city where work is performed to a city where work is not performed, or one who travels from a city where work is not performed to a city where work is performed, should not perform work in either case. But one should not deviate from the local custom if this will lead to dispute" (*Pesachim* 50a). The reason for this ruling, that a visitor is obligated to preclude dispute by conforming to local custom, is that people are not able to tolerate ideas and customs different from their own, and such differences can lead to dispute.

Man's natural aversion to habits and ways of life

that differ from his own is the main cause for strife and infighting, which unfortunately prevails even amongst groups sharing a common purpose. The Sages recognize this aspect of human nature. Seforno writes: "One should try to marry a woman who is fitting for him and who is suitable to become attached to him, for unless the man and the woman are similar to each other, their bond will not be a true bond. If they are similar, they will share the same opinions" (*Seforno*, Bereishis 2:24). Similarly, the Midrash says, "Happy is the man whose wife is from his city" (*Yalkut* Mishlei 5).

In fact, for the sake of *darchei shalom*, it would be advisable for people who have similar habits to live in one vicinity, separate from groups who have differing customs. This premise is implied in *Bava Kama* 82b: "All birds flock with their own species, and men live in the vicinity of those who are similar to them." Similarly, *Sefer HaChinuch* explains that the reason behind the prohibition against ploughing with an ox and a donkey together is that the Torah recognizes the anguish which animals feel when forced to work together with other species. (The "herd instinct," shared by most animals, attests to the truth of this principle.) In conclusion, *Sefer HaChinuch* states that a wise person should apply the principle behind this prohibition to the manner in which he interacts with people. For example, one should not appoint two people of dissimilar personalities to work together — since the Torah recognizes this instinct in animals, it is certainly appropriate to be equally sensitive with human beings.

It is interesting to note that *Sefer HaChinuch* does not differentiate between the animal world's involuntary subservience to instinct and a human being's ability to reason and make ethical evaluations; one's ability to make conscious decisions does not necessarily alleviate subconscious feelings of unease when confronted with habits that differ from his own. This is the reason that the Tribes of Yisrael dwelled in segregation from each other, both in the desert and in Eretz Yisrael. In the times of *Moshiach* this instinct will become transformed, as the verse says, "And the wolf will dwell with the lamb..." (Yeshayahu 11:6-7).

Although the mitzvah of "Love your friend as yourself" (Vayikra 19:18) obligates one to be tolerant of other people's customs, and Mussar works extol the importance of overcoming one's character faults, one should not voluntarily place himself in a difficult situation. This applies to testing one's tolerance of others in the same way as it applies to testing one's resolve against performing idolatry or succumbing to other forms of temptation. Furthermore, by living in the vicinity of people who act differently, one is in constant danger of transgressing the commandment, "Do not harbor hatred for your brother in your heart" (Vayikra 19:17).

The Sages say, "It is prohibited for a man to marry a woman unless he first sees her, lest he will see something displeasing in her; the Torah says, 'And you shall love your friend as yourself' " (*Kiddushin* 41a). This emphasizes the need to have foresight and avoid situations that will necessitate relying on one's resolve and good intentions to overcome difficulties. Instead, one must distance himself from such situations at all costs.

The idea that separation from people who act according to a different code of behavior is commendable, is implied in Rashi's interpretation of the verse, "...And they could not speak to him in peace." (Bereishis 37:4):

"From the guilt of Joseph's brothers we learn of their praiseworthy traits: they were incapable of speaking in one way and feeling opposite emotions in their hearts." Rambam writes, "When a man commits a sin against another, the victim should not hate the sinner in his heart and keep silent, as the verse says concerning evil-doers, 'And Avshalom did not speak to Amnon a single word, neither good nor bad, for Avshalom hated Amnon' (Shmuel II 13:22). Instead, it is a mitzvah to notify him of his sin and tell him, 'Why did you do such and such to me, and why did you sin by committing this transgression,' as the verse says, 'Surely rebuke your fellow man' " (Rambam, *Hilchos De'os* 6:6).

By minimizing close contact with people who have differing customs and who act according to a different code of behavior one may avoid strained relationships. "Anger is better than laughter" (Koheles 7:3). *Metzudos David* explains the meaning of this verse: "If a person commits a sin against another and the latter expresses his anger, this is preferable to his feigning friendliness. Expressing one's anger has the effect of quelling that anger; the heart will become tranquil and the wronged party will not look for revenge. Conversely, if one feigns impartiality *without* forgiving, the feelings of anger will remain buried in his heart — when the opportunity arises, he will not have mercy and will take revenge." Shlomo HaMelech's understanding of man's nature was very discerning!

Chapter 7

Developing Love for Others

The Sages said, " 'Love your friend as yourself' is a general rule throughout the Torah" (*Yerushalmi Nedarim* 9:4). Through his love for others one will refrain from causing them physical or emotional pain; in fact he will work for their benefit and behave towards them with *derech eretz*.

Orchos Tzaddikim writes that it is possible to train oneself to feel love for people. This can be achieved by fulfilling these codes of behavior:

1) Speak gently. If someone embarrasses or misleads you, do not reciprocate.

2) Share other people's burdens and refrain from increasing their suffering. Never conduct heated arguments with others. Welcome everyone joyously and with a friendly facial expression, since a friendly expression strengthens bonds of love.

3) Soothe people who feel worried or angry.

4) Honor others, both verbally and through your actions. Never act in a haughty manner with anyone;

instead, yield to the will of others.

5) Refrain from passing judgment on others; instead, look for the merit in other people's actions.

6) Conduct all transactions honestly.

7) Strive to benefit others, not to benefit from others.

8) Extend help to others, both physically and monetarily. Refrain from miserliness.

9) Avoid speaking in a derogatory manner about others, and refrain from listening to others speak negatively about people.

Being a Good Neighbor

Pirkei Avos states, "One of the ways to which a man must adhere is to be a good neighbor" (2:13). The term "neighbor" refers to any person with whom one is friendly and whom one meets regularly (see page 24, 6). In general, in order to be a good neighbor one must fulfill the aforementioned principles. For example, extend help to others, both physical and monetary (8), strive to benefit others, not to benefit from others (7), share other people's burdens and refrain from increasing their suffering, and never conduct heated arguments with others (2).

Although the obligation to carry on friendly relations with one's neighbor is great, one must not visit a neighbor too often, since overly frequent visits will eventually cause the neighbor to hate the visitor. Concerning this idea, the verse says, "Let your foot be seldom in your neighbor's house, lest he will be weary of you and hate you" (Mishlei 25:17). Rashi explains that just as eating an overabundance of honey makes one feel like vomiting, so, too, frequent visits cause the host to hate the visitor. *Metzudos David* writes that love between people increases when they are absent from each other, whereas overly frequent visits have the opposite effect. The reason for this phenomenon is the human instinct which abhors different habits — a neighbor's close physical proximity emphasizes the existence of those differences. This factor, in combination with a neighbor's overly frequent visits, will inevitably cause feelings of anxiety and hatred to surface. The Midrash assumes that this rule is even applicable between husband and wife; one of the reasons given for the Torah's law that a husband distance himself from his wife at given times is to prevent them from becoming overly familiar with each other and subsequently coming to hate each other.

Chapter 8

Honoring People

Pirkei Avos states, "Who is honored? He who honors others" (4:1). One who honors others indicates that he is respectable. This idea is illustrated by the Midrash (*Bereishis Rabbah* 48:15), which relates that Avraham Avinu deduced that the angels who appeared to him in the guise of human beings were respectable people, from the way they honored each other. Furthermore, we are admonished to honor each other, as it states, "One who knows that his fellow man is greater than himself in even one aspect must honor him, even if he has not learned anything from him" (*Pesachim* 103b).

Honoring People in the Right Measure

It is important to honor each person in a manner befitting him. Showering undue respect on an undeserving person, indirectly causes the honor of deserving people to be reduced.

The Talmud relates that when R. Shimon Ben Gamliel the *nassi* entered the *beis midrash*, everyone stood up; when R. Meir the *chacham* (the *rosh yeshivah*) and R. Nasan the *av beis din* walked in, everyone stood up once again. R. Shimon Ben Gamliel decided to establish a decree which called for different degrees of honor for each of the three posts: When the *nassi* enters, everyone stands up until told to sit down. When the *av beis din* enters, the people should line up in two rows and remain standing until he sits; when the *chacham* enters, everyone must stand when he comes within four *amos*, until he passes.

Sifsei Kohen comments, "Today we do not have a *nassi* or an *av beis din* like they did in their days; every *rosh yeshivah* and *av beis din* should be regarded as a *chacham*" (*Yoreh Deah* 244:15). Other authorities are of the opinion that since each city appoints a Rav to teach and judge over them, he is to be honored in the same manner as the *nassi* was honored.

Honoring *Talmidei Chachamim*

The importance of honoring *talmidei chachamim* is great indeed. The Talmud attributes the death of R. Akiva's students to their unwillingness to honor each other (*Yevamos* 66b). The severity of this obligation is illustrated by the Talmud, which reports that R. Yehoshua's teeth became black as a result of his many fasts to atone for the inappropriate manner of speech with which he once addressed *Beis Shammai* (*Chagigah* 22b).

Honoring Those Who Perform Righteous Deeds and the Wealthy

It is a mitzvah to honor a person who performs kind deeds, even if he is not wealthy (*Kiddushin* 33b).

The verse says, "He who pursues righteousness and kind deeds will find life, righteousness and honor" (Mishlei 21:21). Rashi (*Yevamos* 109b) interprets this verse to mean that a person who performs righteous deeds will also merit to be honored in this world. The Talmud's report that Rebbi used to honor wealthy people (*Eruvin* 86a) illustrates the fulfillment of this verse: He honored them for performing kind deeds.

Honoring a King

There is an obligation to honor any king, even a king of one of the nations. This obligation is derived from the verse, "And Hashem spoke to Moshe and to Aharon, and commanded them concerning the children of Yisrael and Pharaoh, king of Mitzrayim, to bring the children of Yisrael out of the land of Mitzrayim" (Shemos 6:13). Rashi explains that Hashem commanded Moshe and Aharon to honor Pharaoh.

Speaking in the Presence of a Greater Person

The Mishnah (*Avos* 5:10) teaches that refraining from speaking in the presence of a distinguished person is one of the signs of wisdom. The Midrash describes the consequences of speaking in front of a greater person: "Why did Rachel die before her elder sister? Because she spoke in the presence of her sister, as the verse says, 'And Rachel and Leah answered him and they said to him...' (Bereishis 31:14). She was punished even though Yaakov called Rachel first, as the verse says, 'And Yaakov sent word and he called to Rachel and to Leah' " (31:4).

Concerning the explanation of the verse, "Shimon and Levi are brothers..." (Bereishis 49:5), Rashi states that Yaakov suspected Shimon and Levi of having sold Yosef. The reason he suspected them and did not suspect Issachar and Zevulun of having committed this sin is that, "They did not speak in the presence of their elder brothers." Rashi's explanation indicates that this principle of *derech eretz* was assumed as a matter of course by the Patriarchs and their sons.

Honoring While Giving Rebuke

The verse says, "Surely rebuke your fellow man and do not bear sin because of him" (Vayikra 19:17). Sifra states: "Even if one gives rebuke four and five times to no avail, he is obligated to continue to rebuke the sinner. Should he give rebuke even if this will cause embarrassment to the sinner? The verse says, 'Do not bear sin because of him.' " This teaches that it is prohibited to rebuke a transgressor in public if this will cause him embarrassment; however, one is obligated to continue giving rebuke in private (this law is discussed in detail in *Sefer HaChinuch, mitzvah* 500).

Sefer Orach Meisharim (ch. 31) writes that the person giving rebuke should not speak harshly; instead, he should assure the sinner that it is in his own best interests to accept the rebuke. He should speak gently and argue in a logical and sincere manner, thus sparing the sinner needless embarrassment. Furthermore, the purpose of giving rebuke is that the sinner change his ways. Concerning this, the Sages say, "The words of a wise man are heard in gentleness" (Koheles 19:17) — over aggressiveness on the part of the person giving rebuke will have the effect of further entrenching the sinner in his ways.

Rambam is of the opinion that this was Moshe Rabbeinu's sin at the *mei merivah* — he addressed the Jewish people in an angry manner, as the verse says, "Listen, rebellious ones..." (Bemidbar 20:10). Rambam explains that the simplest Jew of Moshe Rabbeinu's generation reached the same level of spiritual awareness as Yechezkel Ben Buzi the prophet. Thus, it was wrong of Moshe to express anger to people of such stature. Furthermore, the Jewish people understandably concluded that Moshe's anger was a manifestation of Hashem's anger towards them; in actuality, Hashem was not angry with them. Thus, in a certain sense, Moshe Rabbeinu was guilty of desecrating the name of Hashem.

Chapter 9

The Importance of Impartiality in Interpersonal Relations

A basic principle of *derech eretz* is to treat every person with equal respect and honor. This type of conduct will have the effect of minimizing feelings of jealousy and competition in others. This is the intention of the Sages' statement, "One must treat his children equally — as a result of Yaakov's gift to Yosef his brothers became jealous. A series of events ensued, culminating in our forefathers' exile to Mitzrayim" (*Shabbos* 10b). Why didn't Yaakov soothe his other sons' feelings when he detected that they were jealous? The answer may be that once Yaakov demonstrated his greater love for Yosef, no words could correct the relationship with his other sons. We may here infer a valuable lesson: The failure to be impartial could lead to bitter consequences, and could destroy close relationships.

This principle of *derech eretz* is even applicable if a child's or student's achievements distinguish him from his peers, as was the case with Yosef. The difficulty of soothing or appeasing a person who has the feeling that he was disfavored is illustrated by the Midrash:

> "The verse says, 'And God made the *two large* luminaries', and another verse says, '...and the small luminary...' (Bereishis 1:16). [This seeming contradiction is explained in the following dialogue:] The moon said to the Almighty, 'Master of the World, can two kings wear one crown?' The Almighty answered, 'Go then, and make yourself smaller.' The moon said, '[Just] because I have expressed a legitimate point, shall I go and make myself smaller?' He said to the moon, 'Go then, and have sovereignty over the day and the night.' The moon answered, 'Of what value is the light of a candle during daylight?' The Almighty said, 'Tzaddikim will call themselves after you: Yaakov the small, Shmuel the small, David the small.' The moon was not appeased. The Almighty said, 'Bring a sacrifice for My sake (the sacrificial goat offered on Rosh Chodesh) to atone for having made the moon smaller' " (*Chulin* 60b).

The Gemara (*Yoma* 12b) states that if the *Kohen Gadol* becomes unfit for performing his duties, the deputy *Kohen Gadol* takes his place. When the *Kohen Gadol* is again fit to resume his duties, the deputy is divested of the duties of a *Kohen Gadol*. The reason behind this law is to prevent the *Kohen Gadol* from feeling usurped by his deputy, a feeling which could foment hatred and competitiveness. This law exemplifies the degree of sensitivity one must develop in order to avoid hurting other people's feelings.

Moshe Rabbeinu displayed just such an exalted degree of sensitivity by refusing to assume the appointment as the Jews' spokesman to Pharaoh, out of concern that his elder brother Aharon would feel envious of him, having been bypassed by Hashem. Similarly, the Gemara *(Sanhedrin* 17a) states that Moshe Rabbeinu appointed an equal number of sages from each tribe in order to preempt feelings of envy which might arise between them.

Chapter 10

Between Parents and Children

The Torah obligates one to honor his parents. However, this conduct is in essence an underlying principle of *derech eretz*. It is accepted by most human beings, even those who do not accept the commandments of the Torah. This is attested to by the fact that Eisav, who was by all standards a sinner, took great care to honor his parents. Similarly, the Talmud acclaims the manner in which Dumah Ben Nesinah honored his parents, even though he was a gentile (*Kiddushin* 31).

The most basic requirement of this mitzvah is a sincere desire to please one's parents. The Sages say, "Some give their father *passioni* [an expensive type of bird] and are nevertheless driven away from this world" (*Kiddushin* 31). Rashi explains that this refers to a person whose facial expression betrays his miserliness, even while serving expensive food to his father. The Sages' statement teaches that the most essential requirement for fulfilling this mitzvah is a pleasant and pleasing attitude.

Some Basic Laws concerning *Kibud Av VeEim*

1) One must always address his parents in a gentle manner.

2) It is prohibited to remind one's parents of favors one has performed for them in the past.

3) One may appoint his mother as his *shaliach* (envoy), but it is prohibited to make such use of his father.

4) When praying for a parent's recovery from illness, one should not attach dignified prefixes to his father's name, such as "my master" or "my teacher" — it is not proper to venerate a person while speaking before Hashem (*Birkei Yosef*). This rule is also applicable when praying for the health of one's Rav.

5) One must honor his stepmother or stepfather.

6) Although a person must respect his parents-in-law, he is not required to honor them to the same degree as his own parents. Instead, he must honor them in the same manner as he would honor a *talmid chacham*.

7) It is an obligation to honor grandparents. Honoring one's own parents takes precedence over honoring one's grandparents if one act precludes the other.

8) The Sages disagree about whether the son of a sinner is obligated to honor his father. The *Aruch HaShulchan* writes that most halachic authorities are of the opinion that such a father is not deserving of honor. However, a father who is not a willing transgressor of sins, but rather a *tinok shenishbah* (a person who did not receive a Torah education), is not considered a sinner. If there is a doubt whether a person is considered a sinner, his son is obligated to honor him.

Chapter 11

Parents and Teenagers

Here is not the place to discuss education of young children, for this is a long and complicated subject unto itself.[2] Rather, we will look at *derech eretz* between parents and older children, from age seventeen or eighteen.

The *Shulchan Aruch* states: "It is prohibited for a person to make heavy demands on his children and to be exacting with his honor. This way he will not cause them to transgress [since it is likely that if he is too demanding they will disobey him]. Instead, he should forgive their offenses and overlook their shortcomings" (*Yoreh Deah* 240:19). A person must accustom himself to avoiding hurting his children needlessly, since one who hurts them for no reason (that is, one who becomes angry with his children without a reason) will have to answer for his sins. In addition, one must not allow himself to become exceedingly angry with his son, since

---

2. See my work, *Successful Chinuch*.

this will surely cause the son to rebel against the father (that is, the son will not be able to suppress the urge to respond in an insolent manner).

The gravity of this matter is illustrated by *Sefer Chassidim*: "If father and son are unable to restrain themselves from quarrelling when in each other's presence, it is preferable that they keep apart from each other [even for extended periods of time]."

It is important to acknowledge a young adult's sense of independence and value his opinions for two reasons: First, because *derech eretz* dictates so, and second, because the failure to do so will increase the possibility that the young adult will rebel against his parents. The parent who follows the aforementioned rule of the *Shulchan Aruch* is indeed wise, since this type of behavior will induce his children to respect his judgment and wisdom.

Relating to a Married Daughter

Parents of a married daughter may not instruct her to perform an action that will in any way interfere with her responsibility towards her husband. According to Torah law, a married woman is not obligated to look after her parent's needs, since her primary obligation rests in fulfilling her husband's will.

Parental Dignity

A parent must not act in a light-headed manner while in the presence of his children; instead, he should retain a dignified appearance at all times. This will cause his children to respect his authority and seek his counsel.

One of the leading authorities of the last generation was particular not to come within sight of his children unless he was dressed in his jacket.

Chapter 12

How Should a Leader Behave?

In reference to the laws concerning Jewish kings, Rambam defines how a leader should perceive his role:

> In the same manner as the Torah accords him [a Jewish king] honor, it also commands him to be modest and unassuming. He should not behave in a haughty manner towards his fellow Jews, as the verse says, "...in order that his heart should not become elevated over his brethren..." (Devarim 17:20). When addressing the congregation, he should speak in a soft manner, as the verse says, 'Listen to me, my brothers and my people' (*Divrei Hayamim* I 28:2). He must conduct himself with extreme humility — no man surpassed Moshe Rabbeinu's achievements, and yet he said, "What are we?" (Shemos 16:8). He must bear their burden, complaints and angry outbursts (*Hilchos Malachim* ch. 2).

If this degree of humility is required of a king then certainly a common person, even a supervisor over hundreds of people, is obligated to act in a humble and unpretentious manner.

In actuality, a person who conducts himself in a self-effacing manner only stands to gain, since people are more likely to be influenced by a humble person than by a haughty one. As the verse says, "The gentle words of the wise are heeded" (Koheles 9:17).

Orchos Tzaddikim explains that one must speak gently when rebuking another person; otherwise, the criticism will not be accepted. If a person senses that he is being affronted, he will naturally recoil and become defensive. The Talmud (*Shabbos* 34a) states that the instructions one must give his family members on *erev Shabbos* (separate *maaser*, make an *eiruv*, and light the candles) should be phrased in a gentle manner — this will induce his family members to follow his instructions.

In another reference, the Talmud states, "A man should not instill a feeling of excessive fear in his home" (*Gittin* 7a). In order to illustrate the importance of this principle, the Talmud relates an incident concerning a man who did just this. His family members once lost one of the limbs of a freshly slaughtered kosher animal; fearing his forthcoming wrath, they substituted the lost limb with a limb from a nonkosher animal. The Talmud concludes that a person who instills fear in his home will eventually transgress a grave sin.

Rashi further illustrates this point, telling how a wife who fears her husband's wrath may feel frightened to inform him that she did not immerse herself in a *mikvah* as planned; instead, she will hide this fact and live with her husband while she is ritually unclean. Further, one who fears her husband's anger may come to light the Shabbos candles or cook food after she accepts the Shabbos.

Benefits of Speaking Gently

1) Most individuals value the privilege of making choices and thereby determine their course of action. For this reason, it is inherently difficult for people to follow orders. A person who gives orders to others must remember this fact and act accordingly. By speaking gently and treating others with respect, one can rest assured that his orders will be executed in accordance with his instructions.

2) The need to speak to people in a kind and gentle manner is absolutely essential when instructing an individual on how to perform a task with which he is unfamiliar. When confronted with a new experience, most people adopt a defensive attitude in a feeble attempt to hide their ignorance. If the instructor's tone of voice or manner of behavior makes the individual feel threatened, the lesson has in effect come to a close — the capacity to internalize information is seriously impaired by the individual's need to protect his self-image.

3) It is self-evident that an employee who is satisfied with his working conditions is more productive than one who is dissatisfied. The employer-worker relationship is one of the essential components of a positive working environment. In light of these facts, any employer with business acumen will readily recognize the financial benefits of treating his employees with respect.

Ethical Obligation to Speak Gently

The verse says, "Did not He who made me in the belly make him? And did not One fashion us in the womb?" (Iyov 31:15). Rambam (*Hilchos Avadim* 9:8) derives from this verse the following rule:

> It is permitted to command an *eved Kena'ani* [non-Jewish slave] to perform hard labor. Even so, piety and wisdom dictate that a person be merciful, pursue righteousness, refrain from increasing his slave's responsibilities, and give him choice portions of food and drink. The Sages of the past used to give their slaves a portion of each dish they ate and each drink they drank. They used to feed their slaves and animals before eating their own meals. Thus, one must not physically or verbally dishonor his slave; although the Torah decreed that they serve as slaves, it did not permit others to degrade them. One must not consistently shout or get angry with his slave; instead, he should speak to him kindly and listen to his complaints.

Anger and impudence are qualities foreign to the Jewish character; they are traits peculiar to idolaters. Avraham Avinu's progeny, upon whom Hashem bestowed the goodness of His Torah, and to whom He commanded His statutes and righteous laws, are merciful towards everyone. This is also a trait of Hashem, Whose ways we are commanded to emulate, as the verse says, "...And His mercy is on all His creations" (Tehillim 145:9).

Although this law concerns non-Jewish slaves, it can also shed light on how one must conduct himself

with his children, his students and all other people with
whom he comes in contact.

Taking Counsel with
People of Lesser Stature

As mentioned previously (page 5), the commentaries explain that the verse, "Let Us make Adam"
(Bereishis 1:26) teaches that Hashem took counsel with
the angels before creating man. From this we learn that
even a person of distinction should always take counsel
with people of lesser stature. The importance that the
Torah attaches to *derech eretz* and humility is apparent
from this verse, as the Torah chose the words — "Let *Us*
make Adam" to teach this concept, despite the fact that
one could wrongly infer from these words that there are
two Heavenly rulers. Rabbi Ben Tzion Bruk *zt"l* ex-
plained that an additional lesson may be derived from
this verse: One must take counsel with people of lesser
stature even if this will result in diminishing one's own
standing.

This does not mean that a person of distinction
should never make his own decisions, since this would
be tantamount to transferring the reigns of power to
those of lesser stature. Rather, the objective is to inform a
person of lesser stature about one's decision before acting upon it, and to consider his criticism. The final decision, however, must be made by the person of distinction.

This idea is illustrated by the Midrash (*Yalkut*
Bereishis 12), which explains that after Hashem informed
the angels of his intention to make man in His image, a
heated discussion broke out in the Heavens. One group
of angels spoke in favor of this decision, arguing that

man's capability to perform kind deeds qualifies him to be created in His image, while another group spoke in opposition, contending that man is full of falsehood. Another group spoke in favor, maintaining that man's ability to act righteously justifies his creation, while still another spoke in opposition, arguing that man's character is essentially disposed to dispute. The Midrash concludes, "Even while the angels debated the wisdom of this decision, Hashem created man."

Even so, one who makes a controversial decision should try to placate those who are in opposition. This is derived from the manner in which Hashem argued in favor of the creation of Man — He assured that man's offspring would be righteous, concealing the fact that wicked offspring would also be born. There are even times when the wisest approach is to simply keep silent. In this manner, others will not disturb him in performing the required action.

Chapter 13

Acting Wisely

The Midrash describes how Avraham Avinu solved a difficult problem: Should he tell Sarah his wife that Hashem commanded him to sacrifice their only son, Yitzchak? And if not, then how should he explain his and Yitzchak's absence? Avraham decided against taking the "straightforward" approach and telling Sarah of his true intention, because women, no matter how pious and righteous they may be, are swayed by their emotions. Notified of the true design, she may have opposed the fulfillment of the mitzvah. Conversely, if Avraham and Yitzchak would have left clandestinely, she would have been terribly worried. Instead, he acted wisely: He said, "Purchase food and drink for us, so that we may celebrate today!" She asked, "What is the reason for this celebration?" He answered, "The fact that old people like us gave birth to a son is enough reason to celebrate!" During the meal he said to her, "You know that when I was three years old I came to recognize my Creator. The youth is growing, and he has not received education. I know of a place where they educate people. Shall I take him there?" She answered, "Take him in peace." Avraham woke early the next morning, saying to himself, "I will leave while she sleeps, lest she change her mind" (*Yalkut* Bereishis 98).

This Midrash teaches a great lesson: Avraham recognized both sides of the dilemma: On the one hand, his obligation to fulfill Hashem's mitzvah, and on the other, his duty to obtain Sarah's consent without jeopardizing his relationship with her or causing her undue anguish. In order to achieve these objectives, he saw the need to utilize deception. He did not assume that his wife, with all her righteousness, would agree to such a fearsome act. He recognized that a woman's decisions are sometimes influenced by her emotions. Thus, he determined that telling Sarah the truth would only make the fulfillment of the mitzvah more difficult.

Often one is confronted with similar situations, especially with one's family members. When these occasions occur, one must resist the initial urge to be "straightforward"; rather, one must determine which of these two approaches will best achieve the goal of fulfilling the mitzvos without alienating one's spouse or children — stating the facts explicitly, or employing altruistic deception. If one is unable to make this decision, he should consult a *talmid chacham*.

Chapter 14

*Honor Others,
Yet Suspect Them*

The Mishnah in *Masseches Derech Eretz* makes the following paradoxical statement: "Regard all men as if they were thieves, yet honor them as you would honor Rabban Gamliel" (*Derech Eretz*, ch. 5). Concerning this Mishnah the Talmud asks, "Has it not been taught, 'Do not judge others until you have stood in their place'?" (*Kallah*, ch. 9). The Talmud answers, "This is not a difficulty. [The first] applies to a stranger, and [the second] applies to an acquaintance."

This Mishnah stresses the idea that one must not close his eyes to reality; one must use his common sense. As the Sages said, "Most people commit the sin of stealing"[3] (*Bava Basra* 165). Since this is the reality, we are

---

3. This is not te be taken literally; it means that most people find it difficult to be scrupulously honest in business.

obligated to take the necessary precautions against falling prey to thieves — we must suspect strangers until we are certain they are trustworthy.

This obligation is equally applicable both to business transactions and to giving *tzedakah*. One must not believe everything he hears. The Sages say, "A poor man who asks for clothes should be investigated, but one who asks for food need not be investigated" (*Baba Basra* 9a). Every individual must consider himself as the treasurer of a charity fund and refrain from giving his money away freely. By giving to people who are not deserving of charity, one in effect supports transgressors and deprives those who are truly in need.

One who conducts himself in the manner of the Mishnah will avoid misunderstandings and needless anguish. *Reishis Chochmah* writes this explicitly: "One must always honor every person; even so, one must guard himself from them and refuse to believe those people whom he does not know" (*Perek Derech Eretz*). The Talmud relates an occurrence that illustrates this concept:

> An incident transpired involving R. Yehoshua, when a person asked him for hospitality. He gave him food and drink, and he brought him to the attic[4] to lie down. He then took away the ladder. The guest awoke in the middle of the night, took objects from the house, and gathered them in a blanket. While attempting to go down [from the attic], he fell and broke his neck. When R. Yehoshua arose from bed, he found the man lying down. He said to him, "Is this what men like you

---

4. Via the loft

do?" He answered him, "Rabbi, I did not know that you took away the ladder." R. Yehoshua replied, "Do you not know that last night I was suspicious of you?"

From this R. Yehoshua derived: "Regard all men as if they were thieves, yet honor them as you would honor Rabban Gamliel" (*Masseches Derech Eretz Rabbah*, ch. 5).

Chapter 15

To Be Concerned

One of the essential principles of *derech eretz* is to help those who suffer. Rabbeinu Yonah writes (*Shaarei Teshuvah* 3:70): "We have been taught to attempt to help our acquaintances, to advise them and to assist them in their time of anguish, as it says, 'You shall not stand aside when mischief befalls your neighbor' (Vayikrah 19:16). If the Torah commands us to care for our neighbor's ox and sheep, then certainly we are obligated to care for *him*. If you have the ability to help him, either through advice or action, and you act as if you are not able to do so, your strength will be taken away; the punishment is proportional to the sin." Thus, Rabbeinu Yonah continues, it is necessary to appoint volunteers in every city who are willing to extend help to anyone who requires it.

In *Iggeres HaTeshuvah* it is suggested that jovial and personable people should be appointed to make peace between Jews, as the verse says, "A soft answer turns away wrath, but grievous words stir up anger" (Mishlei 15:1). David Hamelech prayed that his son Shlomo should have these qualities: "For he shall deliver the needy when he cries; the poor also, and he who has no helper. He will spare the poor and needy, and shall save the souls of the needy. He will redeem their souls from deceit and violence, and precious shall their blood be in his sight" (Tehillim 72:12-14).

The Rambam writes that a king of Israel must possess these qualities: "He must be giving and merciful to meek and great people alike. He must pursue their well-being, and he must respect the honor of even the smallest of the small" (*Hilchos Melachim* 2:6). Rabbeinu Yonah writes in *Shaarei Teshuvah* 3:13: "A man must seek the well-being of his nation and exert himself for the benefit of his fellow Jew, whether he be poor or wealthy. This is one of the most essential and stringent requirements."

Chapter 16

Bending the Truth for the Sake of Peace and Derech Eretz

The degree of importance which the Torah attaches to *derech eretz* is demonstrated by the fact that, in some circumstances, it endorses the use of bending the truth in order to maintain peaceful relations between people. This is derived from the dialogue between the Almighty and Avraham Avinu. When Sarah heard the angel proclaim that she would be blessed with a child, she laughed: "Then Sarah laughed within herself, saying, 'After I am grown old shall I have pleasure, my lord being old also?' " (Bereishis 18:12). When Hashem reported Sarah's reaction to Avraham, however, He modified her words, and said, "Why did Sarah laugh, saying, 'Shall *I, who am old*, indeed bear a child?' " (ibid., 14). Rashi explains that Hashem omitted Sarah's statement, "...my lord being old also," in order to prevent dispute between husband and wife. The Talmud (*Kesuvos* 17a) derives from this verse that it is permitted to congratulate a person for making a wise purchase even if the purchase was in truth unwise; likewise it is permitted to say that an ugly bride is beautiful.

In general, any situation which, if left unchecked, would result in the severance of friendly relations, warrants bending the truth.

Yosef's brothers said to him after their father's death, "...Your father commanded before his death saying, '...Please, pardon your brothers' sin...' " (Bereishis 50:17). Rashi explains that Yaakov never made such a command; he did not suspect that Yosef would harm his brothers. In fact, the brothers fabricated this account in order to ensure their own safety. This teaches that it is even permitted for one of the contending parties to bend the truth if it will help restore harmony.

The Talmud (*Yevamos* 65b) states that it is not only permitted to bend the truth for the sake of *derech eretz*, but it is even a mitzvah to do so. It appears that the Talmud infers this from the fact that Hashem, Who is all-truthful, chose to make a statement which is not true, for the sake of maintaining harmony between man and wife.

The commonly held value that telling the truth is *always* good, and lying *always* bad is not based on the Torah. One's actions must not be dictated solely by his own set of values; instead, one must do whatever is necessary in order to further the objectives of the Torah. R. Saadiah Gaon recognized the error of adhering to one's own set of values. While confessing his sins he used to say, "What You have permitted, I have prohibited to myself."

Escaping Sin through Lying

It is permitted to lie in order to avoid committing a transgression. For example, if someone tries to strike up a conversation which will eventually involve the slander of another individual, one may lie in order to bring the conversation to a close.

The following are specific situations in which one is permitted to lie (*Bava Metzia* 23b):

1) *For the Sake of Humility*: If one is asked whether he is conversant in a tractate of the Talmud, he may answer negatively.

2) *For the Sake of Tznius*: One may lie if he is asked an immodest question.

3) *Guests*: According to the Rambam, it is prohibited for a lodger to reveal the identity of his host. We are concerned that if the host's identity is known, others will take advantage of him. According to Rashi, it is prohibited for a lodger to acclaim his host in public, lest this attract disreputable people to request his hospitality. The verse says, "He who blesses his friend in the morning with a loud voice, it will be counted as a curse for him" (Mishlei 27:14). The Talmud explains that this verse refers to a person who is shown generous hospitality by a host and then, the next morning, sits in the marketplace and says, "May Hashem bless so and so...." Disreputable people who hear his words will ask the host for hospitality and thereby deplete him of his possessions (*Erchin* 16a).

In order to ensure that this does not occur, a guest is permitted to say that his host has not offered him generous hospitality even if the truth is the opposite. (This law is mentioned by the Ramah in *Choshen Mishpat* 262.)

The Talmud in *Erchin* teaches another principle of *derech eretz*: One should not discuss an individual's positive attributes, since eventually the discussion will revolve to his negative traits. Rashi explains that in the midst of praising the individual's commendable traits, one will inadvertently think of this or that negative trait that he has. Alternatively, after hearing about his virtuous traits, others will say, "this is not an accurate description of his character." These rules are discussed at length in the *Sefer Chafetz Chaim* (*klal* IX 1-3).

Chapter 17

The Prohibition against Startling a Person

New or unforeseen situations can cause a person to become alarmed. Therefore, if one wants to ask a favor from someone or influence him in some way, one must always tread lightly so that his words will not cause alarm or startle the other person. For example, one should avoid engaging an acquaintance in a conversation about a complex topic when meeting him by chance in the street or in the *beis midrash*. Rather, the most conducive atmosphere for a serious discussion is created by meeting at a prearranged location during a convenient hour.

This principle is derived from numerous sources. *Masseches Derech Eretz* (ch. 5) states: "One must never enter a friend's house unexpected." The Almighty Himself stood by the portal of Gan Eden and summoned Adam, as the verse says, "And Hashem the Lord called to Adam, and He said to him, 'Where are you?'" (Bereishis 3:9). Rashi explains that Hashem called to Adam to engage him in conversation in order that he should not feel consternation at being punished unexpectedly. We also learn this conduct from the verses, "Where is Hevel your brother?" (Bereishis 4:9), and, concerning Bilam, "Who are those people with you?" (Bemidbar 22:9). Undoubtedly, Hashem knew the answers to these questions. However, He asked them in order to forewarn those whom He addressed of His presence. We must emulate this attribute of the Almighty — before giving instructions to another person, one should first make some introductory conversation with him. By employing this technique, one can rest assured that his words will be heeded.

The verse, "And He called to Moshe, and Hashem spoke to him" (Vayikra 1:1), also illustrates this principle. Why did Hashem first call Moshe and afterwards speak to him? The Torah teaches *derech eretz*: one must not say something to another person unless he first calls to him (*Midrash*). This rule appears explicitly in the *Shulchan Aruch* (*Yoreh Deah* 246:12): A Rabbi should not be asked questions upon his entering the *beis midrash*; one may only approach him after he has settled down.

The Talmud teaches, "One must first give praises to Hashem, and afterwards he may pray" (*Berachos* 32a). This idea can also be applied to interpersonal relationships — before making requests of another person, one should first praise him.

Chapter 18

Obtaining the Permission of the Baal Habais

One must refrain from performing any act, no matter how inconsequential, without first obtaining the explicit permission of the *baal habais* (head of the household). This rule even applies if the act to be performed is a mitzvah. We learn this principle from Moshe Rabbeinu. Even though he was the greatest prophet ever to live, the wisest man in the world, the redeemer of Israel, the vehicle for the performance of numerous miracles, both in Mitzrayim and at the Red Sea, and although he ascended the heavens to receive the Torah, he did not enter the *mishkan* until Hashem called him, as it says, (Vayikra 1:1) "And Hashem called to Moshe" (*Midrash Rabbah*, Vayikra, *parashah* 1).

Similarly, Noach did not dare leave the ark until Hashem said to him, "Go out of the ark" (Bereishis 7:16). Noach said, "I only went in with Hashem's permission; I will not go out unless Hashem permits me to." Chanan-

yah, Mishael and Azariah also understood this principle
— they did not go out of the furnace until Nevuchad-
netzar ordered them to (*Tanchuma, parashas Noach*).

Chapter 19

Refraining from Causing Pain to a Person through One's Speech

It is prohibited to hurt a Jew with one's words, as it says, "You shall not defraud one another; but you shall fear your God, for I am Hashem your God" (Vayikra 25:17). Rashi explains the meaning of this verse: "Here [the Torah] warns against *ona'ah*, that one should not irritate another person...." One must refrain from annoying a fellow Jew even indirectly or inadvertently.

The Talmud (*Bava Metzia* 59b) says that if a man was sentenced to death by hanging by the court, one must never say to one of his relatives, "hang up this towel" — the word "hang" evokes memories of his relative's hanging, which will cause him to become embarrassed. Similarly, the halachic authorities relate that a certain woman was once suspected of having committed adultery in Teveriah. A man called to her "Teveriah, Teveriah!" in public. The authorities ruled that he ask her for forgiveness.

Practical Applications

1) *Orchos Tzaddikim* (*Shaar Hashetikah*) writes: "One who is in the company of a person who suffers from a physical disfigurement or handicap must refrain from speaking about that type of handicap. This rule applies even if the afflicted person is not the subject of the discussion — it is very likely that he would think he is the subject of the conversation, which would cause him to feel embarrassed."

2) If one hears a person make an incorrect statement, he should act as if he did not detect the mistake.

3) "When speaking in the presence of a *baal teshuvah* or a person who once transgressed a precept of the Torah, one must avoid mentioning those sins which the person committed" (*Orchos Tzaddikim*, *Shaar Hashetikah*). This rule is very relevant nowadays, considering the large numbers of *baalei teshuvah*.

4) The Talmud (*Sanhedrin* 84a) prohibits speaking in a derogatory manner about non-Jews while in the presence of a convert. Concerning the verse, "And Yisro rejoiced [*vayichad*] for all the goodness which Hashem had done for Yisrael, whom He had delivered out of the hand of Mitzrayim" (Shemos 18:9), Rashi explains that the word "*vayichad*" is related to the word "*hidudin*" — prickles, meaning that Yisro's flesh became full of prickles, implying Yisro's anguish and resentment over the destruction of Mitzrayim. This is the intention of the popular expression, "Do not degrade a non-Jew while in the presence of a convert" (*Sanhedrin* 94a).

5) One must avoid causing embarrassment to others at all times, even when learning Torah. The Midrash asks, "Why was his name 'Doeg HaAdomi'? Because he

reddened David's face during the study of Halachah" [*Adom* = red] (*Midrash Tehillim* 52:4). For this reason, the Talmud warns against asking a rabbi a question if there is reason to suspect he will not know how to answer. Similarly, the Talmud (*Shabbos* 3b) says, "When Rebbi is studying this tractate, do not ask him a question regarding a different tractate." The posuk says, "...one who makes his way will see the salvation of God." (Tehillim 50:23), that is, one who plans his ways, and knows when to ask and when not to ask his questions will prosper (*Moed Katan* 5b). The Talmud (*Tosefta Sanhedrin*, ch. 7) also warns against asking a Sage a question immediately upon his entering the *beis midrash*; one must allow him time to settle his thoughts.[5]

The mandate to avoid embarrassing a Jew even overrides the fulfillment of a mitzvah. Halachah states that it is permitted for one to wear a *tallis* with non-kosher *tzitzis* in the *beis keneses* in order that he should not feel embarrassed by praying without a *tallis* (*Shulchan Aruch, Orach Chaim* 13:3).

The Sages established numerous decrees in order to prevent people of lesser means from feeling embarrassment. For example, the daughters of Israel exchanged dresses with each other when they danced on Yom Kippur and the fifteenth of Av in order that the daughters of the poor should not feel embarrassed (*Taanis* 26b). The Talmud relates that the wealthy used to bring food to a house of mourning in silver and gold vessels, while the poor carried the food in straw baskets. When it became evident that the poor felt embarrassment, the Sages decreed that everyone must bring the food in straw baskets (*Moed Katan* 8a).

---

5. See also *Chulin 6a; Taanis* 4b.

Decrees were also established to prevent people of lesser education from feeling embarrassment. For example, *parashas bikurim* was not read by a person who offered the fruits even if he knew how to read the *parashah*, but rather by someone else — in this manner, a person who did not know how to read the *parashah* would not feel embarrassment (*Bikurim* 3:7). Similarly, the custom at wedding ceremonies is that the *birkas airusin* and *birkas nisuin* (benedictions recited during the wedding ceremony) is not recited by the groom. This way, a groom who does not know how to recite the blessing will not feel embarrassment (*Even Hoezer* 34 in *Beis Shmuel II*).

Chapter 20

Refraining from Damaging Another Person

A human being is held responsible for damages he caused, even inadvertently, because he should have foreseen the situation and taken the necessary precautions. It is a well-known rule that a human being is even liable for damage he caused during his sleep. If a person falls from a roof on a windy day and, as a result of his fall, damages property, he is required to compensate the damaged party even if the extent of his own injuries far outweighs the amount of damage caused by his fall (*Choshen Mishpat* 378:1,2).

A person is also liable for any damages caused by his property. If a docile ox suddenly goes on a rampage and causes damage to property, the ox's owner is responsible for half the damages. These kinds of laws emphasize man's obligation to ensure that his property does not cause damage to another person's property (*Choshen Mishpat* 389:2).

In this same manner, one must take precautions

against allowing his personality traits to inflict emotional damage on others. One must avoid causing others to feel fright or embarrassment. For example, one should not enter another person's house unexpectedly (*Masseches Derech Eretz*, ch. 5) — the occupants of the house may not be dressed modestly, and consequently his abrupt entrance will make them feel embarrassed. The Talmud also states, "I hate three [types of] individuals, and one of them is a person who enters his friend's house unexpectedly" (*Niddah* 16b). R. Yochanan's opinion is that this law even applies to a person who enters his own house unexpectedly.

The rule to refrain from causing emotional damage is also implied in another reference: "A man should not instill a feeling of excessive fear in his home" (*Gittin* 7a). The Talmud explains that instilling fear in one's home may eventually result in the transgression of a Torah precept (see ch. 12).

For this reason, a father should never frighten a child by saying, "I will punish you by doing so and so to you." *Masseches Semachos* (2:4-6) reports that an incident like this once occurred: A father assured his son that he would soon give him a sound thrashing. The situation culminated in the child committing suicide. The Talmud concludes with these words: "This is the reason the Sages said, 'One should not frighten a child; instead, he should beat him immediately.' "

Chapter 21

Guarding One's Health

The Rambam writes: "It is impossible for man to conceive or come to understand the knowledge of the Creator if he is ill" (*Hilchos Deos* 4:1). When sick, a person is incapable of contemplating profound thoughts. In the same manner, a person who is in pain, or feeling tired or hungry, will find it very difficult to behave pleasantly towards others. It is therefore evident that taking care of one's health is a prerequisite for attaining *derech eretz*. *Orchos Tzaddikim* (*Shaar Ha'ahavah*) emphasizes this point:

> Man is not as strong as rocks, nor are his bones as resistant as copper. Thus, he cannot be constantly active. Sometimes he must rest in order to recover his strength. If his intention when he goes to sleep is to rest his body and soul in order to avoid illness, which would render him incapable of fulfilling God's will, then even his sleep is considered a fulfillment of God's will.

Avoiding Poverty

The Sages say that the distress of poverty can make a person lose faith in himself and in his Creator (*Eiruvin* 41b). The Talmud concludes that one should pray fervently that he be spared from experiencing poverty. From here we learn that a person who faces impending poverty should not stoically await his fate. This is the intention of the verse, "Lest I become sated, and deny You, and say, 'Who is the Lord?' Or lest I be poor, and steal, and violate the name of my God" (*Mishlei* 30:9).

Poverty is a frequent cause of family dispute, as the Sages say, "One should always take care to have food in his home, for many family disputes concern the subject of food" (*Bava Metzia* 59a).

Chapter 22

Making Friends

The verse says, "Two are better than one, because they have a good reward for their labor" (Koheles 4:9). Rashi explains that many types of work cannot be initiated by one person; for this reason, it is advantageous to befriend another person. Ibn Ezra explains that it is prudent to befriend others — if one falls or becomes sick, his friend will help him.

The Talmud recognizes the truth of the popular expression, "My friend or my death" (*Taanis* 23a). *Orach Meisharim* (ch. 22) says, "True and loyal friends are extremely essential to man, whether it be for his physical safety, financial interests, or emotional well-being."

Concerning the study of Torah, the Talmud states: "Form numerous [study] groups and toil over the Torah, for Torah is only acquired by one who belongs to a [study] group. R. Yossi Bar Chaninah said, '...A sword [should strike] those *talmidei chachamim* who sit alone and study Torah. In addition, they become foolish, and furthermore, they commit transgressions' " (*Berachos* 63b).

Mesillas Yesharim warns, "We must recognize that we are simple-minded; our minds are extremely weak, and we are full of ignorance. Thus, we often err." Therefore, it is difficult for one to view himself objectively, to assess his own weaknesses. A friend can help him see his faults more clearly and improve his *middos*.

The Me'iri writes (*Avos* 1:6) that even the wisest of the Sages is obligated to acquire a friend — for others can see aspects of his personality that he is unable to observe himself.

Refraining from Revealing Secrets

One must be careful not to reveal secrets even to his close friends. *Pirkei Avos* states: "Do not tell something that cannot be heard, for it will eventually be heard" (2:5). Rabbeinu Yonah explains the meaning of the *mishnah*: "One must guard himself against the possibility that his secret will be revealed. Therefore, one must not reveal a secret to anyone, even his best friend. One should not even verbalize a secret to himself — as people say, 'the walls have ears.' "

Chapter 23

Maintaining an "Ayin Tovah" (Generous Outlook)

According to Rabbeinu Yonah, an indicative trait of a person who has an *ayin tovah* (a benevolent eye) is generosity. This type of person behaves in a friendly manner towards poor people and projects a feeling of true affection for others. Conversely, a person with an *ayin ra'ah* (a stingy eye) is characterized by miserliness. *Ayin ra'ah* is the root of all negative personality traits; it can lead one to commit myriad transgressions (Rabbeinu Yonah, *Pirkei Avos* 2:14).

Concerning the *mishnah*, "*Ayin ra'ah*...removes a person from the world" (*Avos* 2:1b), Rabbeinu Yonah writes: "There exists [the trait of] *ayin ra* and [the trait of] *ayin ra'ah*. *Ayin ra'ah* refers to a miserly person, while *ayin ra* refers to one who envies other people's possessions. His wish to own others' possessions may harm them, for the vision of the eye is capable of causing damage. Beyond this, he also hurts himself — his unfulfilled wishes cause him to burn with envy."

Avos deRabbi Nasan (ch. 16) expands on this theme:

> As a man looks at his own house and wishes that it
> remain standing, so too should he look at his
> friend's house. As one would not wish that his
> wife be the subject of a malicious rumor, so too
> should he not wish that his friend's wife or chil-
> dren be the subject of malicious rumor. In addition,
> one should not be envious of his friend's scholastic
> achievements. There once was a person who was
> envious of another's scholastic achievements. As a
> punishment, his life was shortened by several
> years. [A distinction should be made between *Ki-
> nas Sofrim*, which leads to self-improvement, and
> *envy*, which leads to self-destruction.]

Chapter 24

Behavior beyond Reproach

The *mishnah* (*Shekalim* 3b) states: "A person must pass the judgment of people in the same manner as he must pass Hashem's judgment, as the verse says, 'And the land of Canaan will be subdued before Hashem; then afterwards you (the tribes of Reuven and Gad) will return and *be guiltless before Hashem and before Yisrael*, and this land will be your possession before Hashem' (Bemidbar 32:22). Another verse says, 'Put away from you a dissembling mouth, and perverse lips put far from you' " (Mishlei 4:24).

This teaches that a person must avoid acting in a manner which will cause others to suspect him of inappropriate conduct, whether it be in his financial dealings or in his performance of mitzvos. As the Talmud (*Chulin* 44b) says, "Distance yourself from unpleasantness and the like."

One must avoid acting in a haughty manner under all circumstances. The *Shulchan Aruch* (*Orach Chaim*, ch.

60) discusses the obligation of a *chasan* to recite *Shema* on the night of his wedding so that he should not seem pretentious by implying that he always concentrates while reciting the Shema. Thus we see that the rule to avoid haughty behavior is even applicable when performing a mitzvah (*Mishnah Berurah* 70:14).

Certain Rabbinical decrees were instituted with this idea in mind. For example, the Sages prohibit hanging clothes to dry during Shabbos — they were concerned that people would come to suspect the person of having laundered the clothes on Shabbos. This is also the reason it was prohibited for the person who collected the coins from the *lishkah* (office) of the *Beis HaMikdash* to wear long garments or long hair — people would suspect him of hiding coins in his garments or hair. He was also required to speak continuously while he gathered the coins — in this manner, people would not suspect him of hiding coins in his mouth (*Shekalim* 3:2). These laws give us a better understanding of how careful one must be in order that people should not suspect him of improper conduct.

There are three essential reasons one must avoid suspicion:

1) It is prohibited to suspect an innocent person of having committed a sin. Therefore, a person who causes others to question his integrity and suspect him is guilty of placing a stumbling block in their way.

2) A person who does not care how others perceive him is considered arrogant and shameless. The Sages said, "A person who feels shame will not soon come to sin" (*Nedarim* 2a). The converse is also true — if he does not care how others perceive him, he will eventually succumb to sin.

3) People are easily influenced by one another. If people suspect that a person is guilty of transgressing a precept, this will weaken their own resolve to refrain from sin. (*Rashi*, Devarim 25:18)

It is told that the Chafetz Chaim himself was negatively affected by his surroundings: The first time he saw a Jew desecrate Shabbos in public, he suffered acute anguish and pain. The following Shabbos, his pain was less severe than it had been the previous week.

A *talmid chacham* must take special care to distance himself from situations which might influence people to become lax in the observance of the *mitzvos*. *Sifsei Kohen* writes that this rule applies to any person who is held in high esteem by his community (*Yoreh Deah* 152:1). *Yad Malachi* writes that a *talmid chacham* must refrain from performing any act which people might consider to be a transgression, even if the act is permissible by law. As the Talmud Yerushalmi says, "[People] learn from wrongdoings, and they do not learn from virtuous deeds" (*Moed Katan* 2:5).

Who Is Suspected of Sin?

The Sages (*Moed Katan* 18b) say that not only a person who has actually committed a particular transgression is suspected by others of having perpetrated that sin, but even a person who just partially committed the sin is suspected. Furthermore, even one who only considered doing the sin is suspected. And even one who felt satisfaction after he witnessed another Jew commit the sin is suspected. This gemara teaches that a Heavenly decree determines who will be suspected of having committed a transgression. This is not simply a punitive measure — rather, the purpose of this decree is to induce the sinner to repent. The Gemara specifies that this principle is only true if the suspected person does not have enemies in that city; however, if he has enemies, we may assume that they are the source of the suspicions, and thus consider those suspicions to be unfounded.

It is unfortunate that in our times slanderers and tale bearers are so prevalent. These tale bearers feign piousness, when in truth they secretly cause untold damage to innocent parties by spreading malicious and false rumors. Equally unfortunate is the fact that people believe their lies — there is a dictum that says, "*Lashon hara* [evil gossip] is always believed" (*Alshich*, Koheles). Alas, this sad situation was predicted by the Sages: "The truth will be concealed during the days preceding *Moshiach*" (*Sotah* 49b).

Chapter 25

Avoid Arousing People's Envy

One must not arouse other people's envy. This principle
is derived from Yaakov Avinu's directive to his sons:
"Now, Yaakov saw that there was grain for sale in
Mitzrayim, and Yaakov said to his sons, 'Why do you
look at one another?' " (Bereishis 42:1). Rashi explains
that although they owned sufficient grain, Yaakov warned
his sons against behaving as though they had sufficient
food, for this type of behavior would arouse the envy of
the sons of Yishmael and Eisav. Similarly, Yaakov warned
his sons against entering Mitzrayim together through
one gate, lest they become affected by the evil eye. Since
they were all handsome and strong, he was concerned
that an observer's envy would become aroused (*Rashi*,
Bereishis 42:5). The *Talmud Yerushalmi* (*Berachos* 4:2) instituted a special prayer to this end: "May it be Your will
that I should not become envious of others, and that
others should not become envious of me."

Orach Meisharim (21:5) states that people should not

wear excessively elegant clothing, even on Shabbos. One should rather wear clothes of average quality. There are two reasons for this: in order not to arouse other people's (friends' and neighbors') envy, and in order to avoid arousing the envy of the Gentiles surrounding us. *Orach Meisharim* quotes the Gemara which says, "R. Papa said: 'If the arrogant [people] will desist, then the enemies will also cease'" (*Shabbos* 139a). Rashi explains this cryptic statement as follows: If the Jewish People will desist from taking pride in beautifying themselves with their forelocks and elegant clothes, then those who instigate hatred against them will also cease to exist.

A person must refrain from displaying his wealth in public or from taking on the appearance of an exceptionally successful person. One who has been blessed with numerous children should not flaunt them in public. The only exception, when one may make a public display of his positive deeds, is when giving charity. However, even this is only commendable if the public pledge will induce others to follow suit. Otherwise, it is preferable to give charity discreetly. It is then self-evident that a person who makes a public pledge must give a large sum of money, since a pledge for a small amount of money will induce other people to donate only small sums.

Chapter 26

Benefitting from Others

The Talmud says, "One who wishes to benefit [from others] should benefit like Elisha" (*Berachos* 10b). That is, despite King Solomon's maxim, "One who hates gifts will live" (Mishlei 15:27), it is permitted for a person in need to accept favors. This rule applies even to a wealthy person, as we may derive from the example of Elisha, who accepted the hospitality of other people despite his wealth. A person who accepts favors from people should try to reciprocate with an act of kindness or, at the very least, by giving a blessing to the giver of the gift.

It is perfectly in order to decline favors. However, if a person expresses a sincere wish to help, and if it is within that person's ability to extend that help, one should accept the favor. As R. Pinchas Ben Ya'ir said, "Yisrael are holy, it is proper to derive benefit from them" (*Chulin* 7b).

It is prohibited to accept hospitality from someone who does not have sufficient food for himself. According to the Rambam, (*Hilchos Teshuvah* 4:4) this is a form of theft. Similarly, it is prohibited to accept a gift from a miserly person who is reluctant about parting with his possessions (*Sotah* 38b).

Chapter 27

Being a Guest

Travelling

1. The Talmud (*Derech Eretz* 4, ch. 5) states: "A person should not leave his Rav or acquaintance without first informing him of his departure." Announcing one's departure is a way of honoring the other person. This type of conduct denotes respect and deference.

2) A traveller should always carry food, even if his destination is nearby.

3) It is a good custom to donate money to charity before embarking on a trip.

4) Immediately upon reaching his destination, a traveller should contact his relatives and inform them of his safe arrival. This will prevent them from worrying about his well-being.

5) When returning from a journey, one should not enter his house unannounced. Instead, one should in-

form his household members when to expect his arrival.

Proper Conduct

The Talmud dictates, "One who enters [another's] house must follow his host's instructions" (*Pesachim* 86b). The *Shulchan Aruch* (*Orach Chaim* 170:5) also decrees that a guest must follow the host's instructions without any objections. For example, one must sit wherever the host decides. One must not object even if the host wishes to honor him. Most halachic authorities agree, however, that a guest who feels satiated is entitled to refuse to eat additional food even if the host insists, if this will endanger his health. One may infer from this rule that if additional eating does not pose a danger to the guest's health, it would be correct to comply with the host's wish.

The Talmud says, "A gracious guest should say [to himself], 'How my hosts inconvenience themselves for me! They serve me so much meat, wine, and delicacies!' What does an ungrateful guest say? "Have they inconvenienced themselves for me? I have eaten one piece of bread and one morsel of food, I have drunk one cup of drink. As a matter of fact, my host did not inconvenience himself for me whatsoever; he only labored for his wife and children. [That is, even if I were not his guest, he would have had to provide food for his family]" (*Berachos* 58a).

Rules concerning Eating

1) Upon entering the host's home, the guest should not request food or drink; instead, he should wait until the host offers him food (*Shulchan Aruch, Orach Chaim* 170:13).

2) The most distinguished guest should be invited to wash his hands first (*Berachos* 46, *Orach Chaim* 165:2).

3) The guest should wait until the host serves himself the first portion of food before reaching for food.

4) If two guests sit at the same table and the host is not present, the more distinguished of the two should serve himself first. A person who reaches for food before a person greater than himself is considered a glutton. This law is also applicable to us, even though nowadays each person is served his own plate (*Orach Chaim* 170:12, *Mishnah Berurah* 28).

Rules concerning a *Talmid Chacham*

1) A *talmid chacham* who arrives in a city should introduce himself by his name and omit the title "Rav." However, if he has reason to believe that as a result of his anonymity he will be treated with disrespect, he may declare himself to be a *talmid chacham* (*Yoreh Deah* 246:21). If he visits a city where he is known, however, he should not declare himself to be a *talmid chacham*. As the verse says, "Let strangers praise you, and not your own mouth" (Mishlei 27:2).

2) *Sefer Chassidim* writes that a *talmid chacham* who stays in a city where he is unknown should engage someone in a discussion of Torah. In this manner, the word will eventually spread that he is a *talmid chacham*.

3) If the people of that city overestimate one's importance and consequently show him excessive honor, he is obligated to inform them of their mistake. He must not accept the honor given to him.

A Guest May Not Invite a Guest

The Talmud (*Derech Eretz Zuta*, ch. 8) states that it is improper for a guest to invite another guest without the permission of the host. Worse still is a guest who causes the host to inconvenience himself.

It is prohibited for a guest to give the host's child food from his portion without the host's permission. Some halachic authorities are of the opinion that this law is not applicable if there is abundant food (*Orach Chaim* 170:19).

Common courtesy dictates that the guest inform his host of when he will arrive and depart.

Halachic Stringencies

Derech eretz dictates that a guest take special care to avoid causing his host embarrassment. Therefore, if a guest who has accepted certain halachic stringencies is served perfectly kosher food which does not fit his exacting standards, he should nevertheless eat the food. It is preferable to be excessively stringent about avoiding causing others embarrassment than to be overly stringent about the laws of kashrus.

This idea is illustrated by the frequently quoted principle that, in certain cases, a food which is prohibited during weekdays because one needs to adopt the more stringent view during the week, is permitted for Shabbos or for serving to guests. In these circumstances, one may not disregard the lenient law and abstain from partaking of these foods, since by doing so, one in effect desecrates the sanctity of the Shabbos. This principle is also applicable in our case.

The *Mishnah Berurah* (170:16) writes that a person who accepts certain restrictions on himself should fulfill these stringencies in private. In all other ways, he must comply with his host's instructions. The *Shaarei Teshuvah* writes that this type of conduct fulfills the verse, "I will walk with innocence within *my* house," and not in other people's houses.

The Prohibition against Changing Lodgings

The Torah prohibits changing lodgings when travelling (*Erchin* 16b), as the verse says, "And he [Abraham] journeyed until the place where his tent was *at first*" (Bereishis 13:3). The Talmud specifies that one must endeavor to lodge at the place to which he is accustomed; he may only desist if he is physically evicted from the premises by the owner of the lodging. Rashi explains the reason for this law: People will say, "How difficult are those two — they could not even manage to live in peace together!"

This rule applies even if one pays rent to the landlord.

To Inquire about the Welfare
of the Host's Wife

The Talmud (*Bava Metzia* 87a) states that the Torah teaches us *derech eretz* from the verse, "Where is Sarah, your wife?" (Bereishis 18:9) — even a male guest should inquire after the welfare of his host's wife. One should not address the host's wife directly, but instead should address his question to the host. Some of the Rishonim, however, contest this law, claiming that it is prohibited to inquire about the welfare of the host's wife. According to these opinions, the aforementioned verse teaches us that a guest should ask only about the *whereabouts* of his host's wife. However, the halachah follows the opinions that require a guest to inquire about the welfare of the host's wife (*Even Haezer* 21:6).

(Note that the commentators make a distinction between asking about the wife's welfare and sending regards to the wife, which is prohibited.)

A Guest Is Indebted to His Host

The *Midrash Rabbah* (Shemos 4) states, "If a person opens his door to a guest, the guest is obligated to honor him even more than his own parents." This is because a parent's concern for his children's welfare is natural; in contrast, if a stranger shows kindness to a person, it is entirely due to his desire to perform a kind deed.

The Midrash states that this principle was exhibited by Eliyahu and Elisha, who revived their hosts' children from death but refrained from reviving their own parents.

Moshe Rabbeinu exemplified this trait. Before accepting upon himself the commandment to go to

Mitzrayim and redeem the Jewish people, Moshe Rabbeinu said to Hashem, "Master of the Universe! I cannot fulfill Your commandment, since Yisro welcomed me and opened his door to me, and I am as a son to him. A person who is shown hospitality is eternally indebted to his host." Thus, Moshe refused to embark on his journey without first receiving Yisro's permission. From this we learn that one act of *derech eretz* takes precedence over the redemption of the entire Jewish People!

Chapter 28

Extending Hospitality and Derech Eretz

A Person Who Requests Food Is Not Investigated

The Talmud (*Bava Basra* 9a) states that a person who requests food should not be investigated to determine whether he is an impostor. The reason he is not investigated is because the delay may cause his hunger pangs to increase in intensity. The verse says, "Is it not to share your bread with the hungry..." (Yeshayahu 58:7). This verse commands us to share our bread with the hungry immediately. However, a person who asks to be supplied with clothing should first be investigated.

If there is no food immediately available, the poor person should not be told to wait; instead, he should be told that efforts are being made to supply him with food.

The *Talmud Yerushalmi* relates an unfortunate incident that stresses the importance of this law: A father was travelling with his daughter. When the daughter said, "Abba, I'm thirsty," he answered, "Wait awhile." Again she asked for a drink, and again her father told her to wait. A short time later, she died. Thus we see how vital it is to tell a hungry person that food is coming.

This rule is one example of the general principle: a person who knows he has food in his pack (or thinks he does) feels less hungry than one who does not. This is demonstrated by the *Talmud Yerushalmi* (*Yoma* 6:4): "An incident occurred when Rav Mana went to visit Rav Chagai on Yom Kippur because he [Rav Chagai] was feeling weak. Rav Chagai said to him, 'I am thirsty.' Rav Mana said to him, 'If you wish to drink, do so.' Then Rav Mana left him. After an hour, Rav Mana returned and asked whether Rav Chagai's thirst was quenched. He replied, 'After you gave me permission to drink, my thirst went away.'"

The Gemara relates that, following the *Musaf* service of Yom Kippur, R. Achah used to announce that anyone who has a child to feed should go and feed him, lest the child's health become endangered (*Yoma* 6:4). This teaches the importance of offering food and drink when the need exists. For example, a guest who arrives during the summer season (in a hot climate) should be offered a drink immediately upon his arrival.

How to Treat Guests

The general rule in *hachnassas orchim* is to empathize with the guest's needs and act accordingly. This applies whether the guest is poor or rich, a relative or a

stranger. The following rules have been collected from
Sefer Chessed leAvraham and *Sefer Chassidim*:

1) It is a mitzvah to go out to greet one's guests.
This is the literal meaning of the words *"hachnassas orchim"* (*Avos deRav Nasan* 7).

2) Because first impressions are so important, a host
or hostess should make sure to receive the guest with a
friendly facial expression and a hearty *"Shalom aleichem."*

3) In her husband's absence, a hostess should not
allow male guests in her house unless she is certain that
they are trustworthy. Even in such a case, the hostess
must take precautions to avoid *yichud* (private seclu-
sion)[6] with her guests. A young woman should not accept male guests in her house under any circumstances
unless her husband leaves only for short intervals.

4) One should serve a guest according to the guest's
standard of living and even a little beyond. A host should
not present himself to his guest as though he were destitute; instead, he should act like a wealthy man (*Reishis
Chochmah, Derech Eretz* 3:40).

5) A host must refrain from telling his problems to
his guest, since the mitzvah of *hachnassas orchim* includes
the obligation to instill one's guest with feelings of cheerfulness and confidence.

6) A host should not feel upset if a guest eats heartily.

7) A general principle of *hachnassas orchim* is to provide a destitute guest with sufficient food to satisfy his
hunger. It is more important to serve nutritional food
than fine delicacies.

8) The *Shulchan Aruch* (*Orach Chaim* 170:4) prohibits

---

6. I.e., by locking the front door. Instead, the door should be
   left open or at least unlocked.

looking at the face of a person while he is eating. We are concerned that he will become embarrassed and consequently refrain from satisfying his hunger.

9) A host must refrain from displaying feelings of anger or miserliness in the presence of his guests. We are concerned that such behavior will discourage them from eating heartily.

10) If a guest makes a statement, the host should not contradict him or argue with him. Similarly, if the guest relates a Torah thought, the host should listen attentively.

11) A host should not ask a guest to relate a Torah thought unless he is certain that he is capable of doing so. Similarly, he should not ask him to lead a Shabbos *zemirah* unless he knows that he has musical talent. This rule is especially relevant if young children are present, since the guest's incompetence could be used by them as a source of ridicule.

12) A host should show his guest his room and the location of the bathroom at an early stage.

13) The *Shulchan Aruch* (167:14) states that the host should serve his guest a generous portion. From here we learn that it may be preferable to serve the food on individual plates rather than in a central serving platter. Taking food from a central platter may make a guest feel overly conspicuous, thus dissuading him from taking additional portions.

14) A host should say, "Everything I do is not enough for my guest."

15) A person who has guests or who makes a *seudas mitzvah* should personally serve the guests. The verse says, "And he [Avraham] was standing by them" (Bereishis 18:8).

The Guest Is the Real Benefactor

Perhaps the most elemental obligation of *hachnassas orchim* is to make a guest feel good about accepting the hospitality offered to him. He should be made to understand that he is the real benefactor — he enables the host to merit in the fulfillment of the mitzvah. Ralbag writes that this may be inferred from the verse, "My Masters, if now I have found favor in your sight, pass not by, I pray, from your servant" (Bereishis 18:3). In addition, the Midrash (*Midrash Rabbah*, Vayikrah 34:10) says, "More than the host benefits the poor person, the poor person benefits the host."

How to Host a Long-Term Guest

Although it is a mitzvah to honor a guest beyond one's means, this rule does not apply if the guest intends to stay for an extended period of time. Instead, the following rules specified by the Midrash (*Tanchuma* Pinchas 17) should be applied:

> The Torah teaches *derech eretz*: The first day the guest is served fine quail. The second day, meat. The third day, fish. The fourth day he is served vegetables. With each passing day the quality of the food continues to decline, until eventually he is served legumes [regular food which the members of the household are accustomed to eating].

In this manner, the host will not feel overburdened by his guest. However commendable it may seem, a host who insists on serving his guest the very best food and drink during his entire stay will inevitably come to resent him in his heart. Thus, it is preferable to serve the guest a more modest diet than to risk feeling contempt for him.

It is told of the Gaon R. Shlomo Eiger that, despite his great wealth, he made an agreement with his wife that she refrain from serving fine delicacies to their guests. However unconventional this may seem, it reveals the magnitude of his wisdom: he foresaw that his wife would assign too much importance to the quality of the food served to guests and consequently would refuse to perform this mitzvah unless such food could be provided.

Hosting Relatives

Concerning Yaakov's stay in Lavan's house, the verse says, "And he stayed with him for one month..." (Bereishis 24:14). The Midrash infers from this verse that one should extend hospitality to a relative free of charge for one month.

Offering Accommodations to a Stranger

Derech eretz dictates that upon seeing a stranger enter a city, one should ask him whether he has a place of lodging. As the Talmud (*Bava Kama* 92a) states, "A stranger who comes to town seeking lodging should be questioned concerning lodging, while one who comes to town accompanied by a woman should not be questioned regarding whether she is his wife or his sister. Avimelech the king of the Philistines failed in this; he did make inquiries regarding Sarah's matrimonial status and eventually brought her to his palace. He was then told by Hashem to return Sarah to her husband — otherwise Avimelech would have died, for he should have learned how to receive a stranger coming to his town, and he did not learn." Rashi explains that the words "he should have learned" refer to *derech eretz*. This teaches us that offering a stranger lodging is an obligation stemming from the principles of *derech eretz*, and not just a praiseworthy fulfillment of *hachnassas orchim*.

The male descendants of the nation of Amon and Moav are not permitted to marry a Jewess as a consequence of their failing to come forth and offer bread and water to the Jewish people when they approached their land (Devarim 23:5).

Chapter 29

Rules concerning Gatherings

1) Upon entering a public gathering, one should greet every person in his vicinity.

2) If distinguished people or *talmidei chachamim* are standing, one may not sit down without first obtaining their permission, as it says, "And Boaz took ten people...and he said, 'Sit...'" (Rus 4:2). The Sages comment that we learn from this verse that it is prohibited for a person to sit before first obtaining the permission of the person held in higher esteem" (*Yalkut* on this verse).

3) One should choose a seat which is appropriate for his status.

4) If one's allotted seat is occupied by someone else, he should be flexible and sit somewhere else so as not to embarrass that person. Moreover, he should not resent that person, even in his heart.

5) It is proper to honor those people who sit adjacent to one's seat.

6) One should maintain a pleasant facial expression

during the entire meal.

Before leaving, one should say *"Shalom"* to everyone.

Allocating Appropriate Seating Arrangements

The Sages say, "The location does not honor the person who sits; rather, the person who sits honors the location" (*Taanis* 21b). Nevertheless, it is of utmost importance to designate seats to one's guests in accordance with their (or their husband's) personal stature and social standing. If the host fails in this task, he may unwittingly cause his guests embarrassment and humiliation. Thus, extensive thought and deliberation should be expended in this assignment for a *simchah* or a wedding meal.

The *Shulchan Aruch* gives some guidelines concerning seating arrangements:

1) An accomplished *talmid chacham* takes precedence over an older man of reasonable Torah knowledge in affairs which involve discussion of Torah topics. An older man of a reasonable standard of Torah knowledge takes precedence over a *talmid chacham* in festive meals and other such events.

2) If the *talmid chacham*'s knowledge is not outstanding and the older person is well advanced in years, then the older person takes precedence in all circumstances.

3) If the *talmid chacham*'s knowledge is not outstanding and the older person is *not* well advanced in years, then if the older man has even a little Torah knowledge, he still takes precedence.

An "older person" in this context does not necessarily refer to a man of seventy years of age. Rather, any person who is one's senior is considered an older person (Rashbam, in reference to the daughters of Tzlafchad, *Turei Zahav* 10).

The Aruch HaShulchan asserts that a *talmid chacham*'s sons must not sit beside their father unless they are *talmidei chachamim* in their own right; they should rather be seated in accordance with their own status.

Chapter 30

Women's Role in Hachnassas Orchim

Women play a much more central role in the fulfillment of *hachnassas orchim* than men do. It is the woman in her home who is charged with preparing the food, setting the table, and serving the meals. The Talmud states that this is why the prayer of Abba Chelkiah's wife was accepted before his own: The wife stays at home and gives bread to the poor, thus benefitting them in a more direct manner than her husband is capable of doing (*Taanis* 23b).

The Talmud (*Yevamos* 70b) explains why the daughters of Amon and Moav were not punished along with the men of these nations — it is the men's custom to go out and offer bread and water, not the women's. Yet the Talmud asks, "Shouldn't the women have offered bread and water to the [Jewish] women?" This difficulty is left unanswered here, but the *Yalkut* (Devarim 23) answers: "*Kol kevudah bas melech penima* — all of a woman's honor is on the inside," i.e., that she stays indoors. This teaches us that womanly modesty must not be sacrificed for the sake of doing kindness.

Some educators today encourage girls to do *chessed* outside of the home, such as collecting charity from door to door. Does this type of conduct not contradict the principles illustrated above?

Chapter 31

Derech Eretz While Travelling

The *Shulchan Aruch* establishes that if two wagons are travelling together and one of them breaks down, the other wagon is obligated to stop and wait until the broken wagon is repaired. Although people no longer travel in horse-drawn wagons, the principle behind this and other related laws is still relevant even in these days of modern technology. Some examples of related laws are:

1) A donkey carrying a load has the right of way over an unloaded donkey.

2) A donkey with a rider sitting on it has the right of way over a donkey with no rider, i.e., with the driver leading the donkey.

3) If two people riding on donkeys travel together, they should interchange the right of way successively.

The general idea behind these laws is to refrain from acting in a selfish and pugnacious manner. Instead, one should strive to accommodate and compromise with people.

The Prohibition against Eating in Public

The Talmud (*Kiddushin* 40b) says that a person who eats in the street, i.e., in a place where people would not normally eat, resembles a dog — an animal which has the quality of humility more than other animals. So, too, a person who eats in public demonstrates his lack of humility. The Talmud rules that a person who eats in public is disqualified from giving testimony. Since he lacks the trait of self-effacement, he will not hesitate to give false testimony and thereby risk public ridicule.

Walking with a *Talmid Chacham*

The *Shulchan Aruch* states: "If three people walk together, the Rav should walk in the middle, the next in stature to his right, and the person of least esteem to his left." The *Rama* adds, "When is the statement, 'There is no obligation to give honor while travelling,' applicable? When each person walks alone [and they then meet each other]. However, if people travel in a group, they are obligated to show honor [to each other]" (*Yoreh Deah* 242:17). The Aruch HaShulchan writes that this law refers not only to one's own Rav, but also to any person who is superior in Torah knowledge.

Practical Applications

1) If two people of equal Torah knowledge travel together, they may walk side by side.

2) One who is less knowledgeable than another should walk on the left-hand side.

Entering a *Beis Kenesses,* a *Beis Midrash,* or a House

1) When two people enter a *beis kenesses* or *beis midrash* together, the person of greater importance should go in first. When leaving the *beis kenesses,* however, the person of least importance may leave first, since there is no mitzvah to leave a *beis kenesses.* The *Birkei Yosef* quotes the opinion of the *gaonim* who contend that the person of greater importance should also exit first when leaving a *beis kenesses.*

2) When entering a house, the *baal habais* should enter first. When leaving the house, the guest should exit first (*Masseches Derech Eretz,* ch. 4). When leaving a house owned by someone else, the person of greater importance should leave first.

Chapter 32

Proper Conduct in Accordance with Derech Eretz

Maintaining a Joyful Attitude

A person who feels happy is more likely to act kindly towards people than one who feels unhappy. In addition, an unhappy person is more likely to respond in a gruff manner to a plea for help. It follows that one should endeavor always to maintain a happy disposition.

Refraining from Being Overly Critical

An overly critical person is liable to succumb to anger. In general, people dislike expressions of anger. This is certainly true of one's family members, who have no choice but to withstand one's bouts of rage. Thus, it is self-evident that a person who succumbs to his anger causes untold damage to himself and to those near to him.

Anger causes a person to commit errors of judgment, which in turn influence him to do things that he would not ordinarily do. Furthermore, an angry person is disinclined to giving charity, performing kind deeds or concentrating while praying.

Acting Responsibly

Society disapproves of unreliable people. Rabbeinu Asher recommends, "Be honest with everyone, even with a Gentile" (*Orchos Chaim* 6:129). *Masseches Derech Eretz* advises, "Love [the word] 'perhaps' and hate [the phrase] 'why not'? [implying throwing caution to the wind]." That is, avoid speaking with certitude unless you are absolutely positive that your statement is accurate.

The Sages say, "The punishment of a liar is that no one believes him even when he speaks the truth" (*Sanhedrin* 99b, *Avos deRav Nasan* 34). The Talmud brings a proof for this statement from the sons of Yaakov — because they did not speak the truth to him about Yosef's supposed death, Yaakov refused to believe their claim that Yosef was alive.

The Prohibition against Divulging Another Person's Secret

An element of loyalty is the ability to guard a friend's secret. A person who divulges others' secrets is considered a slanderer, as the verse says, "...slanders, reveals secrets..." (Mishlei 11:13). Included in this prohibition is the disclosure of any piece of information communicated by another person, without receiving explicit permission from that person to share the information with others. The Talmud (*Yoma* 4b) says, "From where do we learn that it is prohibited to disclose another person's statement unless that person has given permission? From the verse, 'And Hashem spoke to him from the *ohel moed* to say [*leimor*]...' " (Vayikra 1:1). Rashi explains that the Gemara discerns a secondary, non-literal understanding of the word *"leimor"* — *"lo emor,"* literally, "do not say." This law is discussed at length in *Sefer Chafetz Chaim* (*klal* 2: 7:18 and *Hilchos Rechilus klal* 8:5).

Rules regarding an Envoy

Rashi writes: "The Torah teaches us *derech eretz* — do not think that if the one who sent you knows of your deeds, you are no longer obligated to inform him [of the completion of your assignment]. This is the meaning of the verse, '...And Moshe relayed the people's word to Hashem' " (Shemos 19:8). This obligation certainly applies if the person who sent the envoy does not know if the assignment was completed according to his instructions. Thus, in order to avoid causing undue worry to the person who appointed him, *derech eretz* would require the envoy to contact him and supply him with up-to-date information concerning the assignment.

Avoid Encroaching upon Others' Authority

One must take great care to avoid encroaching upon other people's authority. We see that Moshe Rabbeinu at first refused to accept the role of leader of the Jewish people out of concern that Aharon would feel usurped by his brother (as Aharon was already a leader of *Klal Yisrael*). Thus, we see that special sensitivity is required when dealing with people who hold public positions.

The Necessity to Prepare Oneself in Advance

Before meeting a person, one should reflect upon how to behave in his presence, for instance, which subjects to introduce into the conversation and which to avoid. Besides Heavenly assistance, great wisdom is required in order to know how to act with each individual. The Sages recognized the difficulty of this task. For this reason, the prayer, "May it be Your will, Hashem...to distance us from an evil person and an evil companion..." was established.

In some instances, all of one's preparations will prove to be futile. For example, if one must meet a person who is accustomed to speaking *lashon hara*, it is highly unlikely that he will succeed in rejecting all the gossip he will hear. Thus, it is best to avoid such a situation altogether. This idea is illustrated by the following halachah: The *Shulchan Aruch* (*Yoreh Deah* 240:7) rules that a son who is an outstanding *talmid chacham* should not live in the same vicinity as his father if there is concern that the father will fail to give his son the honor he deserves. Thus, the Sages ruled that it is preferable to avoid this awkward situation altogether.

Behaving beyond the Letter of the Law

The Talmud (*Bava Metzia* 30b) states: "The only reason Yerushalayim was destroyed is because they behaved according to the letter of the law." This teaches us that we must act with tolerance and forbearance even when the law is on our side. Regarding the verse, "And you shall teach them the ordinances and the laws, and shall show them the way in which they must walk, and the work they must do" (Shemos 18:20), the Sages say, "[The words] 'the work they must do' mean that they are required to act beyond the letter of the law."

Only when all other alternatives are exhausted should one resort to a *beis din*. Even then, if the dispute concerns a small sum of money and it is within one's financial capability to do so, he should give up the money. However, a poor person may pursue his claim in most cases.

The Merit of Being Consistent

People in general disapprove of inconsistent behavior. It reflects emotional immaturity and a lack of seriousness. This character flaw can be repaired by making an effort to plan one's actions in advance.

Refrain from Laughing at Friends

One should not ridicule his friends, even in jest. Eventually, this bantering will result in hatred, at which point the friendly relationship will come to an end.

It Is Prohibited to Refuse the Bidding of a Person of Greater Importance

If a person of importance were to offer an honor to another person, that person would be in a dilemma: On the one hand, one should refuse honor, but on the other hand, it is prohibited to refuse the bidding of a person of greater importance. The Sages determined that heeding to the instructions of a person of greater importance takes precedence over the obligation to avoid honor (*Pesachim* 96b, *Bava Metzia* 97a).

Following the Advice of the Elders

The Talmud (*Megillah* 31b) states: "If elders tell you 'destroy,' and children tell you 'build,' destroy and do not build, since the destruction of the elders is in actuality building, while the building of children is in actuality destruction." This is exemplified by Rachavam ben Shlomo, who followed the advice of the youngsters; consequently, the Ten Tribes seceded from his kingdom.

The Sages say that *talmidei chachamim* become wiser with age. *Pirkei Avos* states: "A person of forty years of age reaches *binah* (understanding), one of fifty reaches *eitzah* (the ability to give advice)" (5:21). Rashi explains that this is derived from the Levi'im: They concluded their service at fifty years of age; after this age, they assisted their brethren. How did they assist them? By offering them advice.

Additional Rules of *Derech Eretz*

1) Rabbeinu Asher writes in *Orchos Chaim*, "A person should avoid involving himself in another's dispute. Eventually, they will reach accommodation and you will still be involved in the argument." Furthermore, by becoming involved one will invariably make enemies. As Rabbeinu Asher says, "Do not underestimate any of your enemies" (*Orchos Chaim* 5:90).

2) When a person shares his misfortune with others, he should first say, "It should never happen to you" (*Sanhedrin* 104b, based on Eichah 1:12).

3) One should not praise a person excessively, since this may be misinterpreted as empty flattery (*Rashi, Eruvin* 18b and *Rashi*, Bereishis 7:1).

4) A person who is received with undue honor is obligated to inform those honoring him of their mistake. (*Makkos* 12b) Similarly, if a person who lacks the necessary credentials to serve as a practicing Rabbi is offered the position of the Rav of a community, he is obligated to decline (*Shabbos* 119b).

5) The Talmud (*Sanhedrin* 38b) rules that it is prohibited to respond to a Jewish apostate under any circumstances. Similarly, one should not answer a fool unless he asks a Torah-related question.

6) One should not enter someone's house while that person is eating, since people find it embarrassing to eat in the presence of others. (*Tov Yehoshua* 3:2)

7) A person should try to avoid the company of wicked people (*Sotah* 7a). One must endeavor not to live amongst evil people, as the Sages say, "Woe to the wicked and woe to his neighbor" (*Negaim* 12:6). Furthermore, one should not live in the vicinity of a pious *am ha'aretz*

(ignoramus) — he does not fulfill the mitzvos punctiliously, and people adopt his habits (*Shabbos* 63b).

8) One should refrain from inviting friends to his house too frequently — eventually, they will begin to quarrel with him (*Sanhedrin* 100b).

9) The *Tosefta* (*Sanhedrin* 7) states, "A person who enters a *beis midrash* and finds people studying halachah should not join their discussion until he knows which subject they are discussing."

10) A Rav must not jest, eat or drink while in the presence of his students (Rambam, *Hilchos Talmud Torah*).

11) A wealthy person should not be miserly. This is inferred from the verse, "Purchase food from them with silver... for Hashem your God has blessed you with your handiwork" (Devarim 2:6). Rashi explains that in order to acknowledge Hashem's blessing, this verse instructs the Jewish people to behave as wealthy people and not as poor people.

12) A man of average wealth should eat food of lesser quality than he is capable of purchasing, clothe himself with garments in accordance with his financial status, and honor his wife and children beyond his financial capability (*Chulin* 94b).